SOCIAL SERVICES INSPECTORATE

Inspecting for Quality

STANDARDS FOR RESIDENTIAL CHILD CARE SERVICES

A handbook for social services managers and inspectors, users of the services and their families

LONDON: HMSO

First published 1994

ISBN 0 11 321828 1

HMSO

HMSO publications are available from:

HMSO Publications Centre
(Mail, fax and telephone orders only)
PO Box 276, London SW8 5DT
Telephone orders 071-873 9090
General enquiries 071-873 0011
(queuing system in operation for both numbers)
Fax orders 071-873 8200

HMSO Bookshops
49 High Holborn, London, WC1V 6HB
(counter service only)
071-873 0011 Fax 071-831 1326
258 Broad Street, Birmingham, B1 2HE
021-643 3740 Fax 021-643 6510
33 Wine Street, Bristol, BS1 2BQ
0272 264306 Fax 0272 294515
9–21 Princess Street, Manchester, M60 8AS
061-834 7201 Fax 061-833 0634
16 Arthur Street, Belfast, BT1 4GD
0232 238451 Fax 0232 235401
71 Lothian Road, Edinburgh EH3 9AZ
031-228 4181 Fax 031-229 2734

HMSO's Accredited Agents
(see Yellow Pages)

And through good booksellers

CONTENTS

PREFACE

The Social Services Inspectorate has now published a variety of materials in the "Caring for Quality" series and, more recently, in the "Inspecting for Quality" series. These documents have had several purposes and have been used by managers, inspectors, purchasers of services and providers, as well as front-line workers and people who use services and their families.

Although the standards contained in this handbook are based primarily on the relevant legislation, regulation and guidance, they have been informed by the SSI's experience of inspection in this area and by extensive discussions with users and former users of these services and researchers and practitioners in this field. I would like to take this opportunity to record our thanks to all those who have been involved in this work.

We are publishing this handbook in the expectation that it will be of value to social services managers, providers, inspectors, service users and their families and anyone else who shares our interest in ensuring that residential child care services are of a proper standard.

Herbert Laming
Chief Inspector

INTRODUCTION

1.1 This catalogue of standards and criteria was prepared to support the SSI's programme of inspections of residential child care services. In recent years, SSI has adopted an increasingly structured, systematic approach to the inspection process. An important element of this development is the specification in advance of the standards and criteria against which services will be evaluated during the inspection.

1.2 In this context, SSI uses the term "standard" to mean the quality of performance which is required in the management and delivery of social services if service provision is to accord with Department of Health policy and practice guidance. Standards are derived from legislation, regulations and guidance, and current professional understanding (based on research and professional experience) of what constitutes good quality services.

1.3 For residential child care services, the Children Act 1989 is the predominant legislation and many of the standards relate directly to the principles of the Act.

1.4 There is also a substantial body of relevant regulation and guidance. A series of nine volumes was published during 1991. The fourth volume in the series, entitled *The Children Act 1989 Guidance and Regulations: Residential Care,* is obviously the main reference point for these standards.

1.5 From this body of legislation, regulation and guidance, together with an understanding of what constitutes good practice, a total of 36 standards have been specified in relation to residential child care services. For ease of use, they have been grouped under nine headings, referred to as Aspects of Care; namely:

- Purpose and Function
- Children's Rights
- Child Protection
- Care of Children
- Quality of Opportunity
- Child Care Planning
- Premises
- Staffing
- Organisation and Management

1.6 For each of the standards a number of criteria have been specified. "Criteria", in this context, is the term used to describe more detailed and specific statements of expectation about particular aspects of a generally stated standard. For the purposes of inspection, evaluation of a service against a broad standard statement can be problematic. Criteria are used to clarify the different component elements of the standard so that these can be separately identified, giving a clearer account of the extent to which the overall standard is achieved and the elements which would benefit from attention.

1.7 For these standards for residential child care services, the criteria have been grouped under three sub-headings: Outcomes for Children, Home Practices and Management Actions.

<u>Outcomes for Children</u> - As a starting point, how do children (and their families) experience and what do they think about the services they receive and are services achieving positive outcomes for them?

<u>Home Practices</u> - What human and material resources are provided for each home and how effectively does the home use them to achieve the objectives set for it? Are sound child care practices in evidence?

<u>Management Actions</u> - What management arrangements are in place that set the conditions for the organisation, delivery, and monitoring of services. Do they facilitate good child care?

At times, the same issues are identified within criteria under more than one of the headings. This duplication remains to highlight the point that some issues have a different emphasis when approached from a different perspective.

1.8 As the title suggests, this handbook is intended for use by social services managers, inspectors, users of these services and their families. It emanated from planning inspections of residential child care services and SSI has developed an inspection methodology for its own inspections based on these statements. The local authority circular LAC(92)14, issued in November 1992, advised that local authorities are expected to inspect community homes for which they have responsibility along with the inspection of registered (private) children's homes. The circular also expected local authorities to devise their own inspection methodologies based on clearly defined standards. The circular suggested, in outline, the stages that a methodology should identify. This general methodological approach is also discussed in an earlier publication of this series entitled *Evaluating Performance in Child Protection*. A diagram summarising this conceptual framework is included here for convenient reference.

A CONCEPTUAL FRAMEWORK OF THE INSPECTION PROCESS

PLANNING	FIELD WORK	ANALYSING	JUDGING	REPORTING	EVALUATING
Define Inspection objectives and purposes	Obtain and assemble pre field work information	Collate and organise information	Make judgements on quality of services inspected	Formulate conclusions and recommendations	Refine standards and criteria
Establish and make known standards to be applied	Undertake field work	Analyse and interpret evidence		Produce report and follow it up	Evaluate the Inspection process
Ensure defined criteria for each standard		Formulate, validate & refine inspection findings			
Decide on sources of information					
Determine methods to be used and design instruments for information collection					

CHART 1

1.9 The inspection process begins with defining the objectives and purpose of the proposed inspection. This will have a bearing on the next stage of selecting the standards and criteria. An inspection may wish to concentrate on certain issues such as particular aspects of care, or a stage in the delivery of a service.

1.10 This handbook presents a catalogue of standards. It is detailed and is intended to be comprehensive. It is important to be clear that not all standards need to be considered at an inspection. A few may be picked out for consideration or sets may be considered within a rolling programme. However, it is vital that inspectors are absolutely clear which standards are being addressed at any one time and that this is fully understood by everyone involved.

1.11 These standards can also be used by managers to evaluate the services they manage and to identify issues for future development plans. Users of the services and their families can use them as a basis for judging the quality of the services they have received or are receiving.

1.12 To date, SSI has inspected residential child care services in 24 local authorities using these standards and criteria. It is worthy of note that within the process, inspectors have seen examples of good professional and managerial practice and outcomes for children across a wide range of aspects of care which demonstrate that these standards are achievable.

REFERENCES

1 *Children in the Public Care: A Review of Residential Care.* W Utting (1991) HMSO London.
(ISBN 0 11 321455 3)

2 *The Children Act 1989: Guidance and Regulations Volume 4: Residential Care.* HMSO London.
(ISBN 0 11 321430 8)

3 *Choosing with Care. The Report of the Inquiry into the Selection, Development and Management of Staff in Children's Homes.* N Warner (1992) HMSO London.
(ISBN 0 11 321559 2)

4 *The Care of Children: Principles and Practice in Regulations and Guidance* (1989) HMSO London.
(ISBN 0 11 321289 5)

5 *The Quality of Care. A Report of the Residential Staffs Inquiry.* E Howe (1992) Local Government Management Board.
(ISBN 9878 60 7488)

6 *Working Together Under the Children Act 1989. Arrangements for Interagency Co-operation for the Protection of Children from Abuse* (1991) HMSO London.
(ISBN 0 11 321472 3)

7 *Looking After Children: Assessing Outcomes in Child Care. The Report of an Independent Working Party Established by the Department of Health* (1991) HMSO London.
(ISBN 0 11 321459 6)

8 *Corporate Parents: Inspection of Residential Child Care Services in Eleven Local Authorities (November 1992 to March 1993).* Social Services Inspectorate.

9 *Evaluating Performance in Child Protection.* (1993) HMSO London.
(ISBN 0 11 321574 6)

THE USE OF TERMS

Every effort has been made to express both the standards and the criteria in straightforward, non-technical language. For example, the words "purpose" and "function" can be completely understood in terms of their standard dictionary definition. Furthermore, the criteria statements have the effect of clarifying the meaning of the standards statement.

If readers need to clarify the meaning of technical terms associated with child care legislation, reference can be made to Section 105 of the *Children Act 1989* or to Annex E of the *Children Act 1989: Guidance and Regulations Volume 6: Children with Disabilities.*

There remain a few terms which have been used in a particular way in this catalogue for which the following further clarification may be helpful.

Child Care Planning

This term embraces the statutory requirements for making arrangements for children in accordance with Regulation 3 of the Arrangements for Placement of Children (General) Regulations 1991, its associated guidance, and the application of professional knowledge based on published research pertinent to decision making in child care.

Complaints

This term is used to describe representations from children or their families about the quality of care received and should be considered in the context of the Representations Procedures (Children) Regulations 1991 and associated guidance. The complaint may contain possible evidence of child abuse in which case child protection procedures should be separately pursued.

DH Consultancy List and
DFE List 99 (formerly DES List 99)

These terms are explained in the *Children Act 1989: Guidance and Regulations Volume 4: Residential Care,* Chapter 1 Section 34.

Notifications

This term is used in the technical sense of the duty to notify certain authorities of significant events in accordance with Regulation 19 of the Children's Homes Regulations 1991. The word "notify" should be construed as in its ordinary dictionary definition.

Outcomes for Children

This phrase is meant to describe components of care required to meet a child's developmental needs which the child's care providers have succeeded in putting in place. It is similar in usage to the term "intermediate outcomes" used and discussed in Chapter 4 of *Assessing Outcomes in Child Care,* the report of the Independent Working Party established by the Department of Health. HMSO 1991.

Placement

This term is used to describe the provision of accommodation and associated care made for a child in accordance with the expectations of planned decisions in the Arrangements for Placement of Children (General) Regulations 1991 and associated guidance.

Responsible Authority

This term must be understood according to how it is defined in the interpretation given in the set of Regulations appropriate to the context. The responsible authority in relation to a child may be different from the responsible authority in relation to a children's home.

Significant Others

This term is used to include people who are neither parents nor relatives but who have an important place in the life of a child. This may include people who have acquired parental responsibility or whom the responsible authority believe need to be involved in considerations of the child's upbringing. The views of the child are clearly directly relevant to who is regarded as significant. In some cases people whom children consider important may not have a positive influence on their upbringing, in which case, the responsible authority may consider their inclusion in particular events to be inappropiate. The purpose of the phrase is to make sure positive contributors to a child's life are included.

The Catalogue of Standards and Criteria

Statements of Standards and Criteria Outline and Contents.

ABBREVIATIONS

Arr Pl Regs	Arrangement for Placement of Children (General) Regulations 1991
Assess Outcomes	Looking After Children: Assessing Outcomes in Child Care. Chief Inspector's letter CI(93)32.
CA	Children Act 1989
CH Regs	Children's Homes Regulations 1991
Guide Permiss Control	Department of Health Guidance on Permissible Forms of Control in Residential Child Care (LAC(93)13)
Guide Smoke Alc	Department of Health Guidelines on Smoking and Alcohol Consumption in Residential Child Care Establishments (LAC(94)4).
LAC	Local Authority Circular
Misc Amend Regs	The Children (Homes, Arrangements for Placement, Reviews and Representations) (Miscellaneous Amendments) Regulations 1993
Rec	Recommendation(s)
Rep Regs	Representations Procedure (Children) Regulations 1991
Rev Regs	Review of Children's Cases Regulations 1991
Sch	Section
Sec	Schedule
Vol 4	The Children Act 1989: Regulations and Guidance: Volume 4: Residential Care
Wor Tog	Working Together Under the Children Act 1989. Arrangements for Interagency Co-operation for the Protection of Children from Abuse.

1 STANDARD: Children's Services Plan

STANDARD STATEMENT

A1 **The function of the home makes a planned and explicit contribution to an integrated range of services for children within a defined geographic area.**

(CA Sch 2 para 1)
(LAC(92)18)

CRITERIA

OUTCOMES FOR CHILDREN

A1.1 That the range of needs of the children being looked after in the home are consistent with the role of the home as described in the Children's Services Plan.

A1.2 That the histories of children being looked after indicate that their needs have been addressed within a rational and integrated system of services.

HOME PRACTICES

A1.3 That the head of the home and senior staff have access to a written copy of the relevant Children's Services Plan, are familiar with its broad content and are conversant with the specific contribution of the home's function to the overall plan.

A1.4 That the overall function of the home, including admission and discharge arrangements, are consistent with its role within the Children's Services Plan.

A1.5 That the head of home confirms that there was consultation when the plan was drawn up and when it was reviewed and revised.

MANAGEMENT ACTIONS

A1.6 That managers can produce written copies of the Children's Services Plan which includes the home as a component.

A1.7 That the Children's Services Plan has been demonstrably drawn up in consultation with:

- The head of the home in question.
- Local Authorities affected by the plan.
- Health authorities.
- Local education authorities.
- Voluntary organisations.
- The private sector.
- Users of children's services.

A1.8 That the Children's Services Plan sets out the means, including specific agreements, by which children in residential care will receive services from education and health authorities and other local authority departments which take account of the special needs which led to the children being looked after by a local authority.

A1.9 That the Children's Services Plan is consistent with national policy and legal requirements.

A1.10 That the Children's Services Plan addressses the role of residential child care as a positive contribution to the range of services for children.

A1.11 That managers can identify agreed arrangements for reviewing and revising the plan as necessary on a regular basis.

2 STANDARD: Statement of Purpose and Function

STANDARD STATEMENT

A2 **The home has a written statement of purpose and function which accurately describes what the home sets out to do for children, the manner in which care is provided, and how this relates to local plans for children's services as a whole.**

(CH Regs 4)
(Vol 4, 1.16 -1.25)

CRITERIA

OUTCOMES FOR CHILDREN

A2.1 That children confirm that a written statement of purpose and function exists, and that this or a specially prepared information document has been provided for them.

A2.2 That children confirm that their experience of the practices within the home conform to the written statement.

HOME PRACTICES

A2.3 That a readily accessible copy of the statement is found within the home.

A2.4 That this written statement is available to staff, children and families.
(CH Regs 4, Sch 1 Part II)

A2.5 That staff are familiar with its content, understand it, and are able to give examples of its relevance to their practices.

A2.6 That observed practices and facilities conform to the written statement.

MANAGEMENT ACTIONS

A2.7 That managers are able to produce written statements for each home which conform to requirements set out in vol 4.
(CH Regs 4)

A2.8 That these statements contain particulars as listed in schedule 1, part 1 of the Children's Homes Regulations 1991, and be available to persons specified in part 2.

(CH Regs, Sch 1)

A2.9 That managers are able to describe how each statement has been prepared, and subject to review and updating. [Also A1]

A2.10 That managers are able to explain how each home contributes to the SSD's overall plan for children's services. [Also A1]

(Vol 4, 1.2)

B ASPECT : Children's Rights

1 STANDARD: Written information for children

STANDARD STATEMENT

B1 **Children and their families receive easily understood written information about the home, its practices and what to do if they wish to complain.**

(CH Regs 4, Sch 1)

CRITERIA

OUTCOMES FOR CHILDREN

B1.1 That children confirm that they have received written information to help them during their stay in the home.

B1.2 That children confirm they have easy access to information conveyed in display form and find its style and presentation acceptable.

B1.3 That children confirm that staff have explained and discussed its content with them.

B1.4 That children confirm that they understand it and find it helpful.

B1.5 That children know what to do if there is something about the home, or something happens to them, which they do not like.

HOME PRACTICES

B1.6 That the home can readily provide a copy of the written information given to children and others.
(CH Regs, Sch 1 Part II)

B1.7 That this information is written in an easily understood, age appropriate style, and is attractively presented.

B1.8 That, when information is in display form, it is presented in a manner which is respectful of staff and children, is attractive, non-bureaucratic in style and located where access is easy for children but not for casual visitors.

B1.9 That it takes account of children's racial, cultural and linguistic backgrounds.

B1.10 That it is comprehensive and complies with relevant regulations and guidance.

B1.11 That in particular it conveys to children how they can express their concerns when they are unhappy, makes clear their right to complain and how to go about this.
(Vol 4, 5.16)

B1.12 That, in particular, it describes permitted and prohibited disciplinary measures and what actions will be taken should the child run away.
(CH Regs 8, 20)

B1.13 That staff take care to explain and discuss the content with the child, the family and significant others, when the child comes to live at the home.

MANAGEMENT ACTIONS

B1.14 That managers have written policy and procedural guidance on the content and quality of written information for children living in homes.

B1.15 That this contains information on the following:

- purpose and function of the home, in accordance with Regulation 4 and Schedule 1 of the Children's Homes Regulations 1991;
- complaints procedures, in accordance with Representation Procedures Guidance, para 5.16;
- permitted and prohibited disciplinary measures, in accordance with Regulation 8 Children's Homes Regulations 1991;
- procedures to be followed if a child is absent without permission, in accordance with Regulation 20 Children's Homes Regulations 1991.

B1.16 That managers can demonstrate mechanisms for determining that information is provided for children, their families and significant others, is perceived by them as clear, understandable, of good quality and presented in an acceptable manner.

2 STANDARD: Consultation

STANDARD STATEMENT

B2 Children's opinions, and that of their family or significant others, are sought over key decisions which are likely to affect their daily life or their future.

(CA Sec 22, 61, 64)
(Arr Pl Regs 3 (3),(4),(5))
(Rev Regs 7)
(Vol 4 1.88)

CRITERIA

OUTCOMES FOR CHILDREN

B2.1 That children feel they are listened to.

B2.2 That children feel they have a real say in decisions which affect their lives.

B2.3 That children feel comfortable in the way they are consulted, including thc morc 'formal' settings such as reviews.

B2.4 That children feel their views are not automatically subordinated to the views of their family or others.

B2.5 That children feel the views of their parents are taken into account to a proper extent.

B2.6 That, where appropriate, family members feel they are listened to.

B2.7 That, where appropriate, family members feel that they have a real say in decisions which affect the family and the lives of their children.

B2.8 That family members feel comfortable in the way they are consulted, including in more 'formal' settings such as reviews.

B2.9 That children feel they have a genuine say in the way the home is run in matters which affect them.

B2.10 That children feel their voice is heard in group meetings, and that these are not dominated by a vociferous minority.

B2.11 That children feel group meetings are well run.

B2.12 That children convey a sense of easy and good communication with staff in every day matters.

HOME PRACTICES

B2.13 That staff in the home ascertain the views and opinions of children and their families and significant others effectively.
(Vol 4, 2.47ff)

B2.14 That staff create the proper time, circumstances and atmosphere for discussing serious matters with the child, the family and others.

B2.15 That significant discussions, views and opinions expressed are recorded promptly and confirmed as accurate with the child and family or others.
(Vol 4, 2.53)

B2.16 That staff have the knowledge, experience and skills to take account of the religious, racial, cultural and linguistic backgrounds of children and their families, and know when to ask for advice or assistance.
(Vol 4, 2.57)

B2.17 That linguistic, ethnic, and cultural difficulties which may affect communication are resolved to enable full discussion of serious matters, and that interpreters or facilitators are available to assist.
(Vol 4, 2.57)

B2.18 That even on less significant matters views are ascertained, and that care is taken to avoid practice which takes for granted the opinion and views of children.

B2.19 That where consultation with a child's family is inappropriate staff explain to children why this is deemed to be so, and that staff actively pursue consultation with significant others or an independent visitor as appropriate. [Also F3]
(Vol 4, 6.2ff)

MANAGEMENT ACTIONS

B2.20 That managers understand and support the requirement to consult with children and their families, both on decisions for individual children and in relation to plans for the future of homes which affect resident children.

(CA, Sec 22, 61, 64)

B2.21 That managers have issued policies and guidance to staff in the home on consultation with children, their families and others.

B2.22 That managers have a mechanism for ensuring that consultation takes place and is effective.

B2.23 That managers provide training for heads of homes and staff on the practice of consultation.

3 STANDARD: Privacy and Confidentiality

STANDARD STATEMENT

B3 The home and staff respect a child's wish for privacy and confidentiality as is consistent with good parenting and the need to protect the child.

(CH Regs 6, 7(3), 7(5), 15)

CRITERIA

OUTCOMES FOR CHILDREN

B3.1 That children feel they are respected in the way staff address them and interrupt their privacy.

B3.2 That children feel staff of the opposite sex are sensitive to their privacy and personal space.

B3.3 That children confirm that showering and bathing arrangements, the use of toilets, how staff deal with everyday personal matters such as menstruation and washing clothes, respect their privacy.

B3.4 That children confirm that they can write letters, without staff wanting to see what they have written or the content of letters they receive.

B3.5 That children confirm that they can use a telephone with privacy and without prior arrangement with staff.

B3.6 That arrangements as regards siting, convenience and payment for the telephone work to the children's satisfaction.

B3.7 That children know of their right to see their case papers, and know that some confidential information might be kept from them.

B3.8 That children and their family think that the papers about them are being kept properly.

HOME PRACTICES

B3.9 That staff respect children's privacy through the way they address them and seek permission before encroaching on their privacy.

B3.10 That staff have been provided with procedural guidance on privacy, confidentiality, and access to case records, and staff confirm an accurate understanding of these matters.

B3.11 That staff are sensitive to gender issues, particularly when dealing with children of the opposite sex.

B3.12 That this is reflected in the way rooms are entered, the showering and bathing arrangements, the use of toilets, and dealing with everyday personal matters such as menstruation and washing clothes.

B3.13 That children are encouraged to write letters in private, and helped to keep in touch with their family and friends.

B3.14 That the home provides a telephone where it is possible for children to make and receive calls in private without reference to staff. [Also G2]

(CH Regs 7(5))

B3.15 That the siting of the telephone and arrangements for payment are convenient and workable.

(CH Regs 7(5))

B3.16 That the home provides rooms for children to meet privately with parents and others. [Also G2]

(CH Regs 7(3))

B3.17 That the home is provided with cabinets in which confidential case papers can be stored securely and located as unobtrusively as possible.

(CH Regs 14(2))
(Vol 4, 1.153)

B3.18 That children's case papers are held in durable, good quality files capable of subdivision and easy extraction of papers which are confidential to the child.

(Vol 4, 1.153)

B3.19 That these files are kept to a standard which respects their importance for the child.

B3.20 That staff know how to deal with information which they are given in confidence when it has implications for the protection of the child.

MANAGEMENT ACTIONS

B3.21 That managers provide policy and procedural guidance for use in homes on privacy, confidentiality and access to case records in accordance with the legislation.
(Vol 4, 2.85-2.87)

B3.22 That managers have made provision for each home to be equipped with a telephone which can be used by children without prior arrangement with staff and in privacy.
(CH Regs 7(5))

B3.23 That managers have ensured the provision of cabinets in each home in which confidential case papers can be stored securely.
(CH Regs 15(2))
(Vol 4, 1.153)

B3.24 That managers ensure that case papers of children are held in durable files capable of subdivision and which allow easy extraction of papers confidential to the child.
(Vol 4, 1.153)

4 STANDARD: Complaints procedures

STANDARD STATEMENT

B4 **Children know how and feel able to complain if they are unhappy with any aspect of living in the home and that any complaint is addressed seriously and without delay.**

(CA Sec 26(8))
(Rep Regs)

CRITERIA

OUTCOMES FOR CHILDREN

B4.1 That children and, where appropriate their family, confirm that they have been provided with a copy of the complaints procedure.

B4.2 That children (and their families) confirm that the procedure and its purpose were explained to them on arrival and at subsequent intervals during their stay in the home.

B4.3 That children feel that staff treat the complaints procedure seriously and that complaints have been, or would be, treated seriously.

B4.4 That children feel that staff help them to bring distress into the open and have assisted, or would assist, them to formulate a complaint.

B4.5 That those children who relate to an independent visitor feel that the visitor helps them to bring distress into the open, and that the visitor has, or would, assist them to formulate a complaint if they wished.

B4.6 That as far as their experience allows, children feel that serious complaints against staff are, or would be, dealt with properly.

B4.7 That children and their families who have made complaints confirm that they were resolved to their satisfaction, even if not resulting in agreement.

HOME PRACTICES

B4.8 That children, and where appropriate, their families and significant others, receive information on how to complain.
(CH Regs Sch 1(13))

B4.9 That the procedures and their purpose are explained to children, and where appropriate, their family and significant others, when the child arrives to live in the home.

B4.10 That staff treat the complaints procedure seriously and do not feel unduly threatened by it, or play it down.

B4.11 That staff encourage children to bring distress into the open and help them formulate a complaint if appropriate.

B4.12 That appointed independent visitors are familiar with the complaints procedure and encourage and assist children to formulate a complaint should they consider this desirable.

B4.13 That serious complaints against staff are dealt with in a way that balances the need to protect the children with the need to safeguard the interests of staff until consequential disciplinary proceedings are complete.

MANAGEMENT ACTIONS

B4.14 That managers have written policy and procedural guidance on representations and complaints in accordance with legal requirements.
(Rep Regs 3(2), 11)

B4.15 That managers take appropriate steps to ensure that an effective complaints procedure is operative within each home which conforms to the legal requirements.
(Rep Regs)

B4.16 That there are systems in place to monitor the effectiveness of the authority's procedures, and to monitor the incidence and outcomes of complaints.
(Rep Regs 10)

1 STANDARD: Vetting and Surveillance of Staff and Visitors

STANDARD STATEMENT

C1 Children are protected from harm from staff in the home through careful selection and vetting of all staff including volunteers and regular visitors to the home.

(Vol 4, 1.34ff)
(Choosing with Care, Chapters 3, 4, 5)

CRITERIA

OUTCOMES FOR CHILDREN

C1.1 That children confirm that they feel safe in the company of all staff, volunteers and visitors to the home.

C1.2 That children confirm that there are opportunities for them to meet, and express views about, applicants for posts in the home. [Also H1]

C1.3 That children confirm that visitors to the home are regulated through the attention of staff and arc not simply free to come and go.

HOME PRACTICES

C1.4 That when recruitment of staff and the approval of volunteers is delegated to the home, selection and vetting procedures are carried out in accordance with the responsible authority's policy and procedural guidance.

C1.5 That senior staff supervising junior staff during their probationary period are alert to the need to draw unsatisfactory performance or inappropriate behaviour to the attention of the staff member as soon as concern is in evidence and to provide a clear written statement of the standard required.

C1.6 That supervisory staff are alert to the need and understand the procedures which lead to unsatisfactory newly recruited staff not being confirmed in post.

C1.7 That the daily log of the home clearly indicates the names of visitors entering the home and the time and duration of their presence.

C1.8 That staff are familiar with the responsible authority's written guidance on the vetting and surveillance of visitors to the home and understand how it is applied.

C1.9 That staff in the home use all the information available to the responsible authority and other agencies represented on the ACPC about relatives who visit children to decide upon any risks this may present to children and take appropriate precautions.

C1.10 That visitors to the home are received and depart with the knowledge of the staff members on duty.

MANAGEMENT ACTIONS

C1.11 That managers have devised reliable routine administrative procedures to check the names of probable employees, including temporary staff from agencies, against police records and the DH consultancy list. [Also H1]
(Vol 4, 1.34)

C1.12 That managers have devised routine administrative procedures for making similar checks on potential volunteers, regular visitors and independent visitors who will have unsupervised contact with children. [Also H1]
(Vol 4, 1.34)

C1.13 That managers responsible for schools have devised routine administrative procedures for checking the names of probable employees against DFE list 99. [Also H1]
(Vol 4, 1.34)

C1.14 That managers have devised selection methods for care staff which, among other things, test for aptitude, sound judgment, a realistic understanding of the needs of children, an ability to withstand personal stress and a willingness to discuss sensitive personal issues and receive support. [Also H1]
(Vol 4, 1.34)

C1.15 That managers have devised routine methods to secure proof of qualifications of employees as early as possible and at least before the person is confirmed in post. [Also H1]
(Vol 4, 1.34)

C1.16 That managers have devised a method of routinely detecting gaps in the record of education and employment and other discrepancies in application forms, and to seek satisfactory explanations before appointments are offered. [Also H1]

(Vol 4, 1.34)

C1.17 That managers have devised methods of checking declared criminal convictions on application forms against information from police checks. [Also H1]

C1.18 That managers have provided clear policy and procedural guidance for assessing and supporting staff during their probationary period, identifying staff who should not be confirmed in post, and ensuring that appropriate notifications are made. [Also H1]

(Choosing with Care, Rec 36)

2 STANDARD: Child Protection Procedures

STANDARD STATEMENT

C2 Children being looked after receive protection from abuse. All staff, including domestic staff and volunteers, know what action to take if they observe or have reported to them possible evidence of abuse.

(Vol 4, 1.179-1.192)
(Wor Tog)

CRITERIA

OUTCOMES FOR CHILDREN

C2.1 That children confirm that they feel safe from abuse.

C2.2 That children feel that staff are protective and would know what to do if they reported evidence of abuse.

C2.3 That children confirm that they know how to contact their field social worker or a responsible adult whom they feel they could speak to if they were being abused or thought that another child was.

C2.4 That children are aware of the purpose of Childline or other helplines and know how to use these if necessary.

HOME PRACTICES

C2.5 That copies of Area Child Protection Procedures and written procedural guidance are available within the home and to staff.

C2.6 That a copy of *Working Together: Under the Children Act 1989* is available within the home and to staff.

C2.7 That a copy of the *Children Act 1989: Guidance and Regulations: Volume 4: Residential Care* is available within the home and to staff.

C2.8 That staff, volunteers and independent visitors are familiar with these documents.

C2.9 That staff, volunteers and independent visitors know what to do if they observe or have reported to them possible evidence of abuse whether by a member of staff or another child.

C2.10 That the Childline telephone number and that of other relevant helplines are clearly displayed near the telephone(s) for the use of children.

C2.11 That staff training is appropriate to the needs of children who have been abused and the purpose and function of the home.

C2.12 That children who have been victims or perpetrators of abuse are supervised as necessary to reduce the possibility of further abuse to an acceptable level.

C2.13 That staff have skills in caring for and supervising children who have been victims or perpetrators of abuse.

MANAGEMENT ACTIONS

C2.14 That managers have developed and issued, in consultation with the Area Child Protection Committee and consistent with 'Working Together', written procedural guidance for staff, volunteers and independent visitors to the home on action to be taken should possible evidence of abuse be observed or reported to them.
(Vol 4, 1.179, 1.181)

C2.15 That managers have made arrangements for the delivery of induction and on-going training on child abuse awareness and child protection procedures for all staff, including domestic staff and volunteers.
(Vol 4, 1.179, 1.181, 1.190)

C2.16 That managers provide an assurance to staff in homes that any action they take to protect children will be supported subsequently, provided that the action is taken in good faith and is consistent with procedural guidance and child protection procedures.

C2.17 That written procedural guidance for staff acknowledges as real the possibility that children may be abused in the home.
(Vol 4, 1.179)

C2.18 That written procedural guidance concerning abuse to children in homes clearly delineates the need for three strands of investigation as follows:

- child protection enquiries;
- police investigation of crime;
- staff disciplinary investigation.

(Vol 4, 1.186-1.189)

C2.19 That policy and written procedural guidance address action to be taken in the event of observed or a report of possible abuse of one child by another, and that child protection procedures be invoked in respect of both children.

(Wor Tog 5.24)
(Vol 4, 1.184-5)

3 STANDARD: Notifications

STANDARD STATEMENT

C3 **All information of significance to the protection of children in homes is notified to the appropriate authorities external to the home.**

(CH Regs 19)
(Vol 4, 1.166, 1.179)

CRITERIA

OUTCOMES FOR CHILDREN

C3.1 That children confirm that all known incidents of serious harm to either themselves or other children have, to the best of their knowledge, been dealt with fully to a proper conclusion.

C3.2 That children confirm that all incidents which they believe to be misconduct have been dealt with fully to a proper conclusion.

C3.3 That children confirm that no member of staff who to their knowledge has repeatedly engaged in misconduct remains employed in thc homc or in contact with children.

HOME PRACTICES

C3.4 That the head of home and senior staff in the home understand and acknowledge the significance and importance of Regulation 19.

C3.5 That the head of home and senior staff in the home can demonstrate their understanding of the need to notify incidents and how to go about this.

MANAGEMENT ACTIONS

C3.6 That, in accordance with Regulation 19 of the Children's Homes Regulations 1991, managers can demonstrate that staff whose conduct renders them unsuitable to work with children have been promptly notified to:

- the local authority
- the registering authority
- the Department of Health

C3.7 That managers can demonstrate an effective system to ensure that information concerning conduct which renders staff unsuitable is transmitted to staff responsible for making notifications, that these staff receive all necessary information promptly, and that this is checked for accuracy with sources as appropriate.

C3.8 That managers can demonstrate an effective system to link staff discipline and related personnel information to the mechanism for making notifications.

C3.9 That managers have issued written guidance for external management and staff in homes on the existence and workings of the Department of Health consultancy list.

C3.10 That managers are able to give a full, accurate and up to date account of possible or actual staff conduct of all known incidents which renders a member of staff unsuitable to work with children.

C3.11 That such accounts are made available to inspectors upon inspection visits, and that these accounts include progress in the handling and resolution of all known incidents of possible misconduct.

D ASPECT OF CARE : Care of Children

1 STANDARD: Staff Relationships with Children

STANDARD STATEMENT

D1 **Children are cared for by staff who can relate effectively to them and who value them.**

(Vol 4, 1.84-5)

CRITERIA

OUTCOMES FOR CHILDREN

D1.1 That children feel that all staff endeavour to relate to them through positive relationships.

D1.2 That children feel that staff are concerned to assist with:

- issues which concern them arising from living in the home;
- problems in their life which make it necessary that they be looked after.

D1.3 That children confirm that staff spend significant amounts of time talking with them.

D1.4 That children are aware of what is expected of them in terms of conduct and self-control.

D1.5 That children feel that they have an effective say in how the home is run, including matters relating to conduct and control.

HOME PRACTICES

D1.6 That care practices in the home are oriented towards:

- the reasons why children are needing to be looked after in the home;
- the needs of children as individuals.

D1.7 That staff are aware of and comply with guidance on:

- appropriate language
- appropriate touching
- appropriate holding
- appropriate restraint

D1.8 That staff recognise the importance of talking with children.

D1.9 That children and staff regularly discuss issues of conduct and control as a feature of life in the home, so that the need for staff intervention is understood by all.

D1.10 That staff share a common understanding of how conflict between children and staff is dealt with positively in the home.

D1.11 That staff share a common understanding for anticipating and dealing with aggression or violence and common strategies for diffusing aggression and preventing violence.

MANAGEMENT ACTIONS

D1.12 That managers have issued a written statement of values and principles consistent with the Children Act 1989 to guide staff in their task of meeting the care needs of children accommodated in the home.

(Vol 4, 1.20)

D1.13 That managers have taken steps to ensure that staff working in the home have the skills, experience and training necessary to care for the children consistent with the statement of purpose and function of the home.

(CH Regs 5)

2 **STANDARD:** **Permitted Disciplinary Measures**

STANDARD STATEMENT

D2 **Children whose conduct is unacceptable are dealt with in accordance with positive disciplinary measures as approved by the responsible authority.**

(CH Regs 8(1))
(Vol 4, 1.90)
(Guide Permiss Control)

CRITERIA

OUTCOMES FOR CHILDREN

D2.1 That children understand what disciplinary measures may arise as a consequence of any unacceptable behaviour.

D2.2 That children confirm that no use is made of prohibited disciplinary measures.
(CH Regs 8(2))

D2.3 That children confirm that staff try to help them improve their behaviour and not simply react when they misbehave.
(Guide Permiss Control)

HOME PRACTICES

D2.4 That staff in the home are able to demonstrate their understanding of the contents of the written statement of permitted and prohibited measures of control.

D2.5 That staff in the home are able to describe clearly the basis on which they make judgment on interventions necessary to maintain control, and that their approach conforms to DH guidance.
(Guide Permiss Control)

D2.6 That the record of disciplinary measures is available for inspection, fully maintained, up to date and in permanent form.
(CH Regs 8(4))

D2.7 That entries in individual children's case records and the daily log which indicate the use of any disciplinary measures, do not indicate any contravention of Regulation 8(2) or the responsible authority's statement on permitted or prohibited measures of control.

(CH Regs 8(2))

D2.8 That the interaction between children and staff indicates that children are rewarded for the achievement of acceptable behaviour and that permitted disciplinary measures are used effectively.

D2.9 That staff work positively and proactively with children's behavioural difficulties.

MANAGEMENT ACTIONS

D2.10 That managers have issued a written statement covering permitted disciplinary measures for use in the home, which takes into account current DH guidance.

(Vol 4)
(Guide Permiss Control)

D2.11 That this statement emphasises the need to reward children for the achievement of acceptable behaviour.

D2.12 That where sanctions are necessary this statement requires that they are relevant, reasonable and carried out as contemporaneously as possible.

D2.13 That this statement encourages reparation and restitution wherever possible.

D2.14 That this statement indicates the circumstances, and with whose approval, particular disciplinary measures may be taken.

D2.15 That this statement gives guidance on the principles to be observed when an incident necessitates that a staff member has physical contact with a child.

D2.16 That this statement gives guidance on the steps a member of staff should take to prevent a child from running away.

D2.17 That this guidance distinguishes between interventions which involve temporary restriction of liberty or physical restraint, which may be reasonable in the circumstances of a particular incident, and the regular use of such measures as part of a regime which would not be permissible.

D2.18 That this statement requires that the use of permitted disciplinary measures is legibly recorded in a dedicated log book and that each entry includes:

- name of child;
- details of the inappropriate behaviour;
- the nature of the sanction;
- the names of staff present;
- the date of the incident;
- the signature of a person authorised on behalf of the responsible authority.
  (CH Regs 8(4))

D2.19 That this statement clearly defines those measures which are prohibited.
(CH Regs 8(2))
(Vol 4, 1.90)

D2.20 That managers have a system to regularly monitor the use of disciplinary measures in homes, including entries in the dedicated log book and that these be made readily available to inspectors.

D2.21 That managers review annually the appropriateness of approved disciplinary measures and the statement as necessary.

3 STANDARD: Absence of child without authority

STANDARD STATEMENT

D3 **Children who are absent without consent are protected in accordance with written guidance.**

(Vol 4, 1.168)
(CH Regs 20)

CRITERIA

OUTCOMES FOR CHILDREN

D3.1 That each child knows what actions will be taken if they are absent without permission.
(CH Regs 20)

D3.2 That each child knows what action will be taken to prevent them running away.

HOME PRACTICES

D3.3 That the home confirms receipt of written procedures prepared by the responsible authority.
(CH Regs 20)

D3.4 That the home has an effective method for informing staff of the legal basis for accommodating each child in the home.

D3.5 That staff are aware of the implications of this legal basis for the action to be taken for each child.

D3.6 That staff are clear about the measures they may take to prevent a particular child running away.

D3.7 That the home has positive practices for receiving a child who returns, or is returned from running away which encourages the child to want to remain.

D3.8 That a child who runs away is offered an opportunity to speak to a person independent of the home.

MANAGEMENT ACTIONS

D3.9 That the responsible authority has issued written procedures to be followed when a child looked after in a home is absent without permission.

(CH Regs 20)

D3.10 That these procedures specifically address absences of a child accommodated under each of the following circumstances:

- when a child is accommodated by agreement with those with parental responsibility;
- when a child is accommodated under a care order;
- when a child is accommodated under a child protection order;
- when a child is detained under the Police and Criminal Evidence Act 1981;
- when a child is remanded by the court to the care of a local authority;
- when a child is authorised to be detained in secure accommodation by an order made under Section 25 of the Children Act 1989.

D3.11 That these procedures are designed to help children settle.

D3.12 That these procedures provide an opportunity for children to be interviewed by a person independent of the home from which they ran away.

D3.13 That these procedures have been effectively communicated to staff and children in homes.

D3.14 That the statement of permitted disciplinary measures issued by managers includes guidance on the steps staff can take to prevent a child running away.

D3.15 That the responsible authority has a system for monitoring children's absences without permission and that this informs the development of policy and practice.

E ASPECT OF CARE : Quality of Opportunity

1 STANDARD: Religion, race, culture, language

STANDARD STATEMENT

E1 **The home makes positive arrangements to help children observe and preserve their religious, racial, cultural and linguistic identity and heritage.**

(CH Regs 11, 12(3))
(CA Sec 22(5)(c), Sec 61(3)(c), Sec 64(3)(c))

CRITERIA

OUTCOMES FOR CHILDREN

E1.1 That children in the home feel that effective efforts are made with regard to individual children's religious, racial, cultural and linguistic backgrounds.

E1.2 That children have a positive appreciation of the cultural diversity given expression in the home.

E1.3 That children from minority ethnic or cultural backgrounds feel that they are in a positive as opposed to an alien environment.

E1.4 That children confirm that they can practice their religion without undue difficulty or embarrassment.

E1.5 That children confirm that they can dress in a manner appropriate to their religion without undue difficulty or embarrassment.

E1.6 That children from Afro-Caribbean backgrounds confirm that their hair and skin care needs are met without undue difficulty or embarrassment.

E1.7 That children confirm that their dietary needs are met without undue difficulty or embarrassment.

E1.8 That children confirm that they have a choice of meals which allows them to enjoy a range of foods from different racial and cultural backgrounds.

E1.9 That children do not experience racism within the home from:

- staff;
- other resident children.

E1.10 That children can confirm that any reported incidents of racism have been, or would be, dealt with satisfactorily. That children confirm that they receive help in handling their experience of racism.

HOME PRACTICES

E1.11 That recruitment practices result in a staff composition which is sympathetic to the religious, racial, cultural and linguistic backgrounds of the children in the home. That the ambience, decoration and display evident in the home reflects in a balanced way the religious, racial, cultural and linguistic background of the children being looked after.

E1.12 That staff are aware of the religious affiliation of each child and the significance this has for the child and his/her family.

(Vol 4, 1.122)

E1.13 That there are effective arrangements to enable each child to observe his or her religion according to the child's and the child's family's wishes.

(CH Regs 11)

E1.14 That the home allows a child to carry out such observance within the home privately, and without embarrassment.

(Vol 4, 1.123)

E1.15 That there are effective arrangements made for a child of a particular background to meet with others of a similar background when, as a result of the child's residence in the home, this does not occur in the normal course of events.

(Vol 4, 1.123)

E1.16 That staff are aware of the dietary requirements of each child, including those determined by religious and cultural background. [Also E5]

(CH Regs 12(3))
(Vol 4, 1.129)

E1.17 That these requirements are met sensitively without imposition on others.

E1.18 That there is ethnic and cultural diversity positively reflected in the choice of meals offered in the home. [Also E5]

E1.19 That effort is made to help children enjoy cultural expression in dress, music, art and design, customs, and celebrations in a way that is satisfying to children from a particular background, and which widens the experience of all children in the home.

E1.20 That the home caters for special needs for hair and skin care as part of its everyday routine.

(Vol 4, 1.147)

E1.21 That the home caters for special requirements of dress as part of its everyday routine.

(Vol 4, 1.147)

E1.22 That children have access to staff able to help children from minority ethnic groups deal with their experience of racism.

E1.23 That the staff are able to describe how racism within the staff group is dealt with effectively.

MANAGEMENT ACTIONS

E1.24 That managers can demonstrate the way in which those sections of the Children Act 1989 which require that due account is taken of a child's religious, racial, cultural and linguistic background have been formulated in the agency's policies, procedures and guidance to staff in the home.

E1.25 That managers communicate these to heads of home and staff in homes, and have means for monitoring their implementation and usefulness.

(Vol 4, 1.39)

E1.26 That programmes of training available to staff in the home address these issues.

E1.27 That managers have recruitment policies which take these issues into account. [Also H1]

E1.28 That there are clear policies and procedures for dealing with allegations and evidence of racism and other forms of discrimination by staff.

(Vol 4, 1.39)

2 STANDARD: Leisure and activity

STANDARD STATEMENT

E2 **Children have ample opportunity to engage in purposeful and enjoyable activities.**

(Vol 4, 1.87)

CRITERIA

OUTCOMES FOR CHILDREN

E2.1 That children do not claim with good reason to be bored.

E2.2 That children confirm that they frequently talk with and do things with staff in the home.

E2.3 That children confirm that part of their leisure time is given over to purposeful activity.

E2.4 That children confirm that trips out to events for enjoyment or interest are encouraged or organised by staff.

E2.5 That children read for pleasure and interest according to their ability.

E2.6 That children talk about hobbies or interests.

E2.7 That children with particular leisure interests confirm that they have been helped to pursue them.

HOME PRACTICES

E2.8 That the staff in the home take steps to engage children in purposeful activities suitable to their age and inclination.

E2.9 That staff show an enthusiasm for talking with, doing things and sharing experiences with children.

E2.10 That the home is not dominated by the television.

E2.11 That means exist for different choices of entertainment from the radio, music system, and television to be accommodated.

E2.12 That children are allowed to do nothing in particular at times, but that alternative choices are on offer.

E2.13 That cultural pursuits are encouraged.

E2.14 That the home receives daily broadsheet and tabloid newspapers, and age appropriate books, magazines and comics.

E2.15 That leisure interests are considered at child care planning meetings and reviews.

MANAGEMENT ACTIONS

E2.16 That managers have negotiated with local facilities opportunities for staff in the home to engage children in activities.

E2.17 That managers have allotted an adequate budget for the home to fund suitable activities for children being looked after in the home.

3 STANDARD: Education

STANDARD STATEMENT

E3 **The home actively promotes the education of children as valuable in itself and as part of their preparation for adulthood.**

(Arr Pl Regs 4 and Sch 3)
(Rev Regs 5 and Sch 2(7))
(Vol 4, 1.105ff, 2.33ff)

CRITERIA

OUTCOMES FOR CHILDREN

E3.1 That children feel that their education is important and that they feel they are encouraged and helped to get the best out of educational opportunities.

E3.2 That children confirm they have an appropriate setting in which to study and do homework.

E3.3 That children confirm that necessary educational books and other requisites are purchased.

E3.4 That children confirm that there is a particular member of staff who takes a special interest in their education, and who encourages and promotes their educational progress.

E3.5 That children confirm that staff from the home attend open evenings and other school or college events.

E3.6 That children feel that they receive help and encouragement with educational activities, projects and homework.

E3.7 That children feel they receive good advice about education and careers.

E3.8 That children feel they can go to a member of staff with worries about their school or college work.

E3.9 That children and their parents feel that they are sufficiently involved in promoting their education.

E3.10 That children with evident special educational needs confirm they are receiving specialised education, and that this conforms to the recorded statement of need as set out in the case records.

E3.11 That children feel that their educational needs are dealt with in a way that is non-stigmatising and respects their wishes and dignity.

HOME PRACTICES

E3.12 That the home conveys an ethos of valuing education and encouragement to children in their education.
(Vol 4, 1.106, 2.33)

E3.13 That staff are familiar with the educational histories and the educational needs of children in the home.
(Arr Pl Regs 4(1) and Sch 3)

E3.14 That case records contain each child's educational history, including details on progress and particular achievement.
(CH Regs Sch 2)

E3.15 That case records reveal a clear written plan which addresses the educational needs of each child.
(Arr Pl Regs 8 and Sch 3)

E3.16 That for each child there is effective contact between home and the school.
(Vol 4, 1.109)

E3.17 That the home takes positive steps with schools to achieve educational continuity for each child.

E3.18 That arrangements are made, wherever possible, to keep children at, or to return them to, their own school.

E3.19 That, for each child, there is an identified member of staff who takes 'parental' responsibility to be personally aware of progress at school and to attend school functions.

E3.20 That there are funds available to purchase educational books and other requisites.

E3.21 That parents are effectively engaged, where and when appropriate, in promoting the education of their child whilst being looked after.

E3.22 That staff encourage and help children with school activities, projects and homework.

E3.23 That each child has an appropriate setting in which to study or do homework. [Also G3]

MANAGEMENT ACTIONS

E3.24 That managers have established effective mechanisms to alert the local education authority and schools to the educational needs of children being looked after.
(Arr Pl Regs 5(1)(c))

E3.25 That managers ensure there is effective inter-departmental co-operation with the education authority in accordance with Sections 27 and 28 of the Children Act 1989.

E3.26 That managers have taken reasonable steps to ensure that there is effective inter-departmental co-operation with the education authority, with particular regard to psychological assessments, the identification of need and the provision of special education as appropriate for children in homes.
(Arr Pl Regs 4(1), Sch 3)

E3.27 That managers have issued written policy, procedures and guidance emphasising that high priority be given to the promotion of the education of children being looked after.
(Vol 4, 1.106-7)

E3.28 That managers have made budgetary allocations to homes for the purchase of educational books and requisites.

E3.29 That managers provide training opportunities for staff in homes on promoting the education of children.

4 STANDARD: Health

STANDARD STATEMENT

E4 The home is energetic in promoting the health care of each child.

(Arr PL Regs 7)
(Rev Regs 6 and Sch 3)
(Vol 4, 1.92ff, 2.23ff)
(Guide Smoke Alc)

CRITERIA

OUTCOMES FOR CHILDREN

E4.1 That children feel their health is important and that they are helped to grow up healthily.

E4.2 That children feel that their health needs are dealt with in a way that is non-stigmatising, respects their feelings and their wish for privacy.

E4.3 That children with evident need for medical, dental, ophthalmic or psychiatric attention confirm that they are receiving it.

E4.4 That children confirm that there is a particular member of staff who has special responsibility to ensure that their health needs are dealt with.

E4.5 That children feel that they have a member of staff with whom they can confide concerning a health worry.

E4.6 That children confirm that they receive health advice and education which will strengthen their understanding and ability to cope with particular dangers, such as smoking, alcohol, substance abuse, sexual abuse, sexually transmitted diseases, HIV/AIDS etc.

E4.7 That children confirm that they are consulted and that the consent of older children is sought for medical examinations or treatment.

E4.8 That children aged 16 or over are aware of their right to consent to or refuse medical examination or treatment, and that younger children are aware that their wishes will be taken into account provided a doctor considers them competent.

E4.9 That children from minority ethnic groups feel their particular health needs are being given proper regard.

HOME PRACTICES

E4.10 That staff are familiar with the health histories and health needs of children in the home.

E4.11 That staff are aware of the particular health needs of children from minority ethnic and cultural groups, and have access to specialist advice when necessary.
(Vol 4, 1.98, 2.26)

E4.12 That case records contain a clear and complete sequence of medical and health information on each child covering as many years as possible, and at least since the child commenced being looked after, unless the child, being of 16 years of age or over, and of sufficient understanding, has not consented to medical examinations.
(Arr Pl Regs 4, 7, Sch 2)
(CH Regs 15, Sch 2)

E4.13 That case records indicate that health assessments for each child have been carried out in accordance with regulatory requirements.
(Arr Pl Regs 7)
(Rev Regs 6)

E4.14 That case records have clear written plans covering preventative measures, dental, vision and hearing and developmental checks, specific treatment or remedial programmes and regular medical assessment in accordance with regulatory requirements.
(Rev Regs 5, 6, Sch 3)

E4.15 That the home has ensured that the health needs of individual children are pursued vigorously.

E4.16 That parents and significant others are engaged, when appropriate, in promoting the health needs of the child whilst in the home.
(Vol 4, 1.98, 1.103)

E4.17 That wherever possible arrangements have been made for children to retain, or return to, their own G.P.
(Vol 4, 1.96)

E4.18 That programmes of prevention and health education, which address issues such as smoking, alcohol, substance abuse, sexual behaviour, sexually transmitted diseases, HIV/AIDS, hygiene, etc. are made available to children in the home.
(Vol 4, 1.95)

E4.19 That staff do exercise effective controls over substance abuse, smoking, drinking and sexual behaviour.

E4.20 That staff behave responsibly and set good examples in these respects.

E4.21 That staff do not smoke whilst on duty.
(Guide Smoke Alc)

E4.22 That there is a general rule that children under 16 years of age are not permitted to smoke.
(Guide Smoke Alc)

E4.23 That children under 16 years of age who are habituated to smoking are actively supported to give up the habit with professional help as necessary.
(Guide Smoke Alc)

E4.24 That smoking in the home (by young people aged 16 or over and visitors) is restricted to a designated room(s) which is not a key room(s) for the communal life of the home.
(Guide Smoke Alc)

E4.25 That the consumption of alcohol is limited to infrequent festive or special occasions.
(Guide Smoke Alc)

E4.26 That no alcohol is stored on the premises.
(Guide Smoke Alc)

E4.27 That staff present as good role models as far as health and coping with disability are concerned.

E4.28 That issues of personal hygiene are dealt with sensitively and with the preservation of the child's dignity.
(Vol 4, 1.143, 1.150)

E4.29 That staff are aware that older children should be consulted and their consent sought for medical examination and treatment, and that children aged 16 and over may refuse such consent.
(Vol 4, 1.104)

MANAGEMENT ACTIONS

E4.30 That managers have ensured that the various components of the local health services are alert to the special health needs of children being looked after, and provide positive support to identify and eliminate any health deficits, in accordance with Section 27 of the Children Act 1989.

E4.31 That managers have issued written policy, procedures and operational guidance on promoting the health of children being looked after for the use of staff in the home.
(Vol 4, 1.94, 2.23ff)

E4.32 That this includes arrangements for the transfer of health information and continuity of treatment for children.
(Vol 4, 2.29)

E4.33 That managers have issued appropriate policy statements and guidance on smoking and the consumption of alcohol in children's residential care establishments.
(Guide Smoke Alc)

E4.34 That managers provide training for staff in homes on promoting the health of children being looked after.

E4.35 That health education advice, having regard to age and understanding, on issues such as smoking, alcohol and substance abuse, sexual behaviour, sexually transmitted diseases, HIV/AIDS, hygiene, etc. is made available to children in the homes.
(Vol 4, 1.95)

5 STANDARD: Provision and preparation of meals

STANDARD STATEMENT

E5 Children are provided with adequate quantities of suitably prepared food having regard to their needs and wishes and have the opportunity to shop for and prepare their own meals.

(CH Regs 12)
(Vol 4, 1.136)

CRITERIA

OUTCOMES FOR CHILDREN

E5.1 That children confirm they enjoy the meals.

E5.2 That children confirm that they eat at least some of their meals together with other children, and that they regard these meals as a positive social event.

E5.3 That children consider there is sufficient quantity and choice.

E5.4 That children confirm they are consulted about menus and the times of meals.

E5.5 That children confirm that there is cultural diversity in the menu.

E5.6 That children experience shopping for food.

E5.7 That children confirm they have opportunities to prepare their own food.

E5.8 That children who are able have opportunities to choose and prepare their own food, go shopping, invite friends to eat, or choose to eat alone, if they so wish.

E5.9 That children with special dietary requirements confirm that their needs are met without fuss or embarrassment.

HOME PRACTICES

E5.10 That the home's routines for the purchasing of food, preparation and consumption of meals are flexible, and involve children.
(Vol 4, 1.130, 1.133)

E5.11 That children help to decide menus.
(Vol 4, 1.128, 1.130)

E5.12 That children go shopping for food as part of the routine of the home.
(Vol 4, 1.136)

E5.13 That meals are orderly, well mannered, pleasant social occasions.
(Vol 4, 1.133)

E5.14 That individual preferences are catered for, and children are encouraged to try new dishes.
(Vol 4, 1.128)

E5.15 That food is provided in adequate quantities, is well prepared and presented, and is wholesome and nutritious.
(CH Regs 12)

E5.16 That there is reasonable choice at each meal, and that menus are varied.
(Vol 4, 1.129)

E5.17 That meals served have regard to the cultural, racial and religious expectations of the children, and represent the ethnic culinary richness of the community. [Also E1]
(Vol 4, 1.125, 1.129)

E5.18 That children may prepare their own snacks.
(Vol 4, 1.130)

E5.19 That there is suitable and sufficient catering equipment, crockery and cutlery available to provide for the needs of children accommodated in the home.
(CH Regs 12(4)(a))

E5.20 That there is proper facility for the refrigeration and storage of food.
(CH Regs 12(4)(b))

E5.21 That in large homes (more than 10 children) the design, layout, equipment, working practices of the kitchen satisfy standards laid down in food hygiene and food safety legislation and the Health and Safety at Work Act 1974.
(Vol 4, 1.137ff)

E5.22 That in small homes (under 10 residents) kitchen facilities are available for use by children, under appropriate supervision.
(CH Regs 12(4)(c))
(Vol 4, 1.139)

E5.23 That in larger homes, where a non-domestic kitchen is required, there is domestic style equipment available for children to use.
(Vol 4, 1.139)

E5.24 That staff responsible for food preparation confirm that they have received adequate and appropriate training.
(Vol 4, 1.140)

E5.25 That a significant number of meals take place in a socially rewarding manner appropriate to the group.
(Vol 4, 1.133)

MANAGEMENT ACTIONS

E5.26 That managers have devised delegated systems to enable staff and children to purchase food and provisions through normal shopping arrangements.

E5.27 That managers have issued policy, procedures and guidance to heads of homes concerning the provision and preparation of meals, with regard to:

- dietary requirements, including those arising from health, religious persuasion, racial and cultural backgrounds; [Also E1]
- consultation with children on choice of meals and timings of meals;
- arrangements, including supervision, for children to purchase and prepare their own food;
- compliance with food safety and hygiene legislation;
- the design, layout, types of equipment, maintenance and safety requirements and working practices in both domestic and non-domestic scale kitchens;
(Vol 4, 1.125ff)

E5.28 That there are arrangements for Environmental Health Officers and catering advisers to inspect, report and advise on food preparation practices in children's homes.

(Vol 4, 1.141)

E5.29 That there is follow up to ensure compliance with any recommendations which arise from such inspections.

E5.30 That appropriate staff receive training in food preparation and hygiene practices.

(Vol 4, 1.140)

E5.31 That managers ensure that systematic and regular checks are made upon catering equipment to ensure that it is safe and in good working order.

6 STANDARD: Children's Personal Appearance

STANDARD STATEMENT

E6 **Children are guided and able to make their own suitable choices with regard to their clothing and appearance.**

(Vol 4, 1.143ff)
(CH Regs 13)

CRITERIA

OUTCOMES FOR CHILDREN

E6.1 That children feel comfortable with what they are wearing.

E6.2 That children confirm that they have been able to exercise choice in purchasing clothes, sanitary protection and toiletries.

E6.3 That children confirm that they are offered guidance with their appearance from adults.

E6.4 That older children, in settled circumstances, have control over monies for clothing and decide where and what to purchase.

E6.5 That young women confirm they have their own personal supply of sanitary protection.

HOME PRACTICES

E6.6 That the head of home and staff in the home are aware of their delegated purchasing responsibilities.

E6.7 That the head of home and staff in the home ensure that children have choice and opportunity in the purchase of clothing and personal requisites through normal shopping arrangements.
(Vol 4, 1.148)

E6.8 That older children, in settled circumstances, have the opportunity to take complete responsibility for control of monies and purchase of items.
(Vol 4, 1.149)

E6.9 That staff advise children on the use of toiletries, cosmetics and sanitary protection.

(Vol 4, 1.145-1.147, 1.150)

E6.10 That staff encourage children to exercise their preferences and manage their personal care independently.

(Vol 4, 1.144-5)

E6.11 That young women have their own personal supply of sanitary protection.

(Vol 4, 1.150)

E6.12 That staff are aware of the significance of a child's religious, cultural and racial background for their choice of clothing and personal requisites.

(Vol 4, 1.146-7)

MANAGEMENT ACTIONS

E6.13 That managers have devised delegated systems to enable staff and children in homes to purchase clothing and personal requisites through normal shopping arrangements.

(Vol 4, 1.143)
(CH Regs 13(1))

E6.14 That managers ensure that any delegated budgets are properly accounted for and monitored.

E6.15 That managers have mechanisms to ensure that children are well clothed.

(Vol 4, 1.143)

E6.16 That managers have a means of ensuring that delegated responsibilities are used constructively with children, and in a way which offers them real choice.

F ASPECT OF CARE : Child care planning

1 STANDARD: Placement of children

STANDARD STATEMENT

F1 There is a written plan to promote the welfare of each child.

(Arr Pl Regs 3, 4, 5, Schs 1, 2, 3, 4)

CRITERIA

OUTCOMES FOR CHILDREN

F1.1 That children have a sense of the purpose of their placement in the home.

F1.2 That there has been discussion of this either before children's admission or very shortly afterwards.

F1.3 That the child care plan addresses the developmental needs of each child and defines clear developmental objectives to be worked on and aimed for.
(Assess Outcomes)

F1.4 That children of appropriate age and ability have been consulted in the process of drawing up the plan.

F1.5 That family and significant others have been consulted in the process of drawing up the plan.

F1.6 That children of appropriate age and ability have seen and read the plan, and have an opportunity to question or amend it.

F1.7 That the plan has been explained and discussed with them by staff.

F1.8 That appropriate special approaches are adopted to explain and discuss plans with very young children or children whose ability to understand is impaired.

F1.9 That any child's disagreement with the written plan has been dealt with constructively.

F1.10 That children are satisfied that all those who need to know about the plan have been informed.

HOME PRACTICES

F1.11 That the home has an up to date written plan for each child drawn up before, or immediately after, the child comes to live at the home.
(Vol 4, 1.152)
(Arr Pl Regs 3)

F1.12 That this plan gives a clear indication of the purpose and aims of the placement, developmental needs and objectives and any other arrangements the home should be working to with the child.
(Arr Pl Regs Sch 1)
(Assess Outcomes)

F1.13 That staff use the plan to provide clarity with regard to the expectations of the home, the expectations of the family and significant others, and the expectations of other agencies, in determining the child's future.
(Vol 4, 1.156)

F1.14 That this plan clearly sets out the arrangements for the child to have contact with family and significant others.
(Arr Pl Regs Sch 1)

F1.15 That this plan is used to promote active participation of family and significant others in decision-making.
(Vol 4, 2.10ff)

F1.16 That the home has regard to the child's educational and health needs, in particular any remedial action to address deficits, in accordance with the plan.
(Arr Pl Regs Sch 2, 3)

MANAGEMENT ACTIONS

F1.17 That managers have written operational procedures to ensure the responsibilities set out in the Arrangements for Placement of Children (General) Regulations 1991 are carried out.
(Vol 4, 2.9)

F1.18 That, in drawing up these procedures, managers have taken account of the importance of writing child care plans which address children's developmental needs and set developmental objectives. [Also F2.25]
(Assess Outcomes)

F1.19 That managers have made clear the respective responsibilities of field and residential staff for drawing up these plans.

F1.20 That there is an effective mechanism for monitoring to ensure that staff understand their responsibilities, and that placements in homes are properly planned.

2 STANDARD: Child care reviews

(For reviews of children's health, see Health)

STANDARD STATEMENT

F2 **Each child's care is subject to formal, systematic and regular review.**

(Rev Regs 2, 3)

CRITERIA

OUTCOMES FOR CHILDREN

F2.1 That children and their families confirm that their involvement in the review process is effective.

F2.2 That children and their families confirm that they are aware of the purpose of reviews, and of the manner in which they are conducted.

F2.3 That children confirm that they are consulted before reviews, do not feel pressured into going along with the views of staff, and know that they can take an independent line if they so wish.

F2.4 That, having regard to their age and understanding, children confirm that they are given advance copies of any written material prepared for the review, in sufficient time to consider and discuss what is written.

F2.5 That children feel supported if they wish to take a line which conflicts with that of their parents or significant others.

F2.6 That children confirm that they are helped to consider the merits of proposals which conflict with their own wishes.

F2.7 That children regard reviews and the need to work to plans as a positive contribution to their development and growing up.

F2.8 That children and their families are aware of specific developmental objectives which are being worked towards.
(Assess Outcomes)

F2.9 That children know the identity of the member of staff with responsibility for progressing the decisions of reviews.

F2.10 That children confirm that they regard the person who chairs reviews as approachable and having a meaningful role in their lives.

F2.11 That children confirm that parents, family members and significant others are engaged appropriately with the review process.

F2.12 That children and families and significant others confirm that the home takes an appropriate role in facilitating their involvement in reviews.

HOME PRACTICES

F2.13 That reviews on children in the home are administered and conducted effectively.
(Vol 4, 3.8ff)

F2.14 That reviews occur on each child within four weeks of commencement of being looked after, again within three months, and, thereafter, not less than every six months.
(Rev Regs 3)

F2.15 That the head of home is clear about who is responsible for initiating and organising reviews.
(Rev Regs 4(2), (3))

F2.16 That whenever this responsibility is undertaken by somebody outside the home, that the head of home ensures that the contribution of the home is taken fully into account.

F2.17 That reviews take place within the home in a way that is sensitive to the feelings of the child concerned, and with minimum disruption to other children.
(Vol 4, 3.18, 3.15)

F2.18 That records show that reviews have taken place within the required time limits.
(CH Regs 15 Sch 2(17))
(Rev Regs 3)

F2.19 That reviews effectively update the child care plan, and clarify and specify care tasks for the home, the child, the family, and significant others.
(Vol 4, 3.19-3.21)

F2.20 That reviews take account of the importance of addressing children's developmental needs and setting developmental objectives.
(Assess Outcomes)

F2.21 That the records of reviews set out measurable objectives and timescales.

(Vol 4, 3.23)

F2.22 That review outcomes are written in plain language, easily understood by staff, the child, family and significant others.

(Vol 4, 1.160)

F2.23 That the names, roles and status of people contributing and named in review write-ups are clearly identifiable by readers unfamiliar with participants.

F2.24 That the home assumes responsibility for preparation for a review in particular by supplying information to participants, and in preparing the child.

F2.25 That there is a key worker system or equivalent which identifies the member of staff who will lead on pursuing plans for a particular child.

MANAGEMENT ACTIONS

F2.26 That managers have produced written policy, and operational guidance for use by the head of home and staff in homes on the requirements for reviewing children looked after.

(Rev Regs 4)
(Vol 4, 3.8)

F2.27 That, in drawing up this policy and operational guidance, managers have taken account of the importance of reviews addressing children's developmental needs and setting developmental objectives. [Also F1.18]

(Assess Outcomes)

F2.28 That there is an officer of the responsible authority appointed to assist in the co-ordination of such reviews.

(Rev Regs 4(3))

F2.29 That there are effective mechanisms in place to monitor compliance with regulations.

(Rev Regs 9)
(Vol 4, 3.26)

F2.30 That in the case of voluntary or private homes there are agreed arrangements for the conduct of reviews drawn up in writing with Local Authorities responsible for looked after children in the home.

(Rev Regs 4)

3 STANDARD: Contact

STANDARD STATEMENT

F3 **Children are looked after in a manner which stresses, and practically supports, contact with parents, family and others of significance to them.**

(Vol 4, 4.9-10)

CRITERIA

OUTCOMES FOR CHILDREN

F3.1 That children confirm that they are encouraged and helped to maintain or restore contact with their parents, family and significant others in accordance with care plans and associated agreements.

F3.2 That independent visitors have been appointed for children who do not enjoy contact with parents, relatives or others of significance to them.

F3.3 That children convey that the home is, for the time being, a positive base from which to live their lives within a wider network of relationships which are significant for the child's future.

F3.4 That children confirm that they have the facilities to keep in touch with family and others of significance.

F3.5 That children confirm that they can receive visitors in comfort and privacy.

HOME PRACTICES

F3.6 That staff actively pursue opportunities to promote or restore contact between the child, parents and significant others in accordance with the individual child's care plans and associated agreements.
(Vol 4, 4.9)

F3.7 That staff facilitate contact, permitted in the arrangements for placement, between the child, family members and significant others immediately the child is admitted, by telephone, arranging early visits or written communication.
(Vol 4, 4.10)

F3.8 That staff exploit the particular advantages of residential care in promoting contact between a child and family.

F3.9 That facilities for receiving visitors are made welcoming through the provision of comfortable furniture and suitable decor maintained to a good standard.
(Vol 4, 1.64-5, 4.18)

F3.10 That staff involve themselves in planning and facilitating visits to enable contact to be positive for the child and family.

F3.11 That visits to a child are supervised only to an extent necessary to safeguard the child and other children in the home.

F3.12 That staff respond positively when children cannot have contact with their parents, members of their family or significant others to help them understand and come to terms with this.

F3.13 That staff are alert to the need to identify children for whom an independent visitor should be appointed. [Also B2]
(Vol 4, 6.2ff)

MANAGEMENT ACTIONS

F3.14 That managers have written guidance for staff in homes which clarifies the rights of children, parents and others for contact having regard to the different legal bases for the child being looked after.
(Vol 4, 4.26)

F3.15 That managers have provided training for staff in homes to develop skills and understanding needed to promote contact.
(Vol 4, 4.21)

F3.16 That managers have ensured that homes have the facilities necessary to foster positive contacts for children.
(CH Regs 7(3), (5))
(Vol 4, 1.64-5)

F3.17 That managers have systems of monitoring the effectiveness of homes in promoting contact.

F3.18 That managers have established effective means for appointing independent visitors when necessary. [Also B2]

4 STANDARD: Preparing for adulthood

STANDARD STATEMENT

F4 **Children in the home receive care which helps prepare and support them into adulthood.**

(CA Sec 24, 61(1)(c), 64(1)(c))
(CH Regs 10)
(Vol 4, 1.115ff, Chapter 7)

CRITERIA

OUTCOMES FOR CHILDREN

F4.1 That children convey that they are being prepared for adulthood in a way that is appropriate to their age and understanding.

F4.2 That children who are "leaving care" have received information on available help.

F4.3 That children who are "leaving care" confirm that staff are enabling them to prepare for this.

F4.4 That they feel the process of preparation allows them to express any concerns and worries.

F4.5 That children anticipating leaving the home are able to describe their involvement in making plans for their future.

F4.6 That they feel these plans adequately address what they are facing.

HOME PRACTICES

F4.7 That staff are aware of the policy and procedural requirements as contained in guidance.
(Vol 4, 7.19ff)

F4.8 That staff are engaged in the preparation of children for adulthood by:

- enabling children to build and maintain relationships;
- enabling children to understand their own sexuality and to establish positive caring sexual relationships;
- enabling children to develop their self-esteem;
- preparing children for the world of work and the possible need to cope with unemployment;
- teaching practical, daily life knowledge and skills.
- teaching financial knowledge and skills.

(Vol 4, 7.43, 7.56)

F4.9 That staff directly assist children who are "leaving care" to find suitable accommodation.

F4.10 That for children who are about to "leave care" an explicit plan for preparation and support, produced with their full participation, is in place.

(Vol 4, 7.18)

F4.11 That staff are allowed and enabled to maintain contact with children who have left the home for whom such contact is significant.

MANAGEMENT ACTIONS

F4.12 That managers have issued a policy statement on the preparation and subsequent support of children "leaving care" in accordance with Section 24 of Children Act 1989 and associated guidance.

(Vol 4, 7.19ff)

F4.13 That this statement has been prepared in consultation with other agencies and shows what relevant services are available from all agencies.

(Vol 4, 7.21)

F4.14 That managers have agreed arrangements with housing authorities and housing agencies for the accommodation of vulnerable young people when they cease to be looked after by the Local Authority in accordance with Section 27 of the Children Act 1989.

F4.15 That a guide is provided for the use of children "leaving care".
(Vol 4, 7.25)

F4.16 That managers have issued procedural guidance for staff in homes and that this requires early preparation of children, and acknowledges the lengthy process of transition and the need for after care, contact and assistance to at least age 21.
(Vol 4, 7.20)

F4.17 That local authority guidance makes explicit its policies and procedures for determining financial or other assistance in kind.
(Vol 4, 7.26)

5 STANDARD: Professional support for the home

STANDARD STATEMENT

F5 **Work with children in the home is positively supported by field social workers and other professionals.**

(CA Sec 27)
(Arr Pl Regs)
(Rev Regs)

CRITERIA

OUTCOMES FOR CHILDREN

F5.1 That children understand the respective roles of the professionals who visit the home.

F5.2 That children understand the role of professionals who work directly with them, either at the home or elsewhere.

HOME PRACTICES

F5.3 That staff in homes are confident about their own role and its relationship with field social workers and other professionals who support the work of the home.

F5.4 That the assigned role of residential social workers gives full recognition of their close contact with, and special understanding of children, and affords them proper status.

F5.5 That the work of professionals external to the home complements the work of staff in the home.
(Vol 4, 1.38, 1.47-48)

F5.6 That the external professionals understand the practicalities of the residential care of children.
(Vol 4, 1.38, 1.47-48)

F5.7 That there are written agreements or contracts which clearly define the roles and expectations of external professionals.

MANAGEMENT ACTIONS

F5.8 That managers have negotiated constructive interagency co-operation in accordance with Section 27 of the Children Act 1989.

F5.9 That managers have written policy and procedural guidance which clarifies the respective roles of field social workers, other professionals and the staff of the homes.

6 STANDARD: Children's Individual Case Files

STANDARD STATEMENT

F6 **Each child has a permanent, private and secure record of their history and progress which can, in compliance with legal requirements for safeguards, be seen by the child, and by the child's parents as appropriate.**

(CH Regs 15, Sch 2)
(Vol 4, 1.152ff)

CRITERIA

OUTCOMES FOR CHILDREN

F6.1 That children have reasonable access to their records.

F6.2 That children confirm they have seen their individual case record.

F6.3 That children understand the purpose and content of their case record.

F6.4 That children make use of their records by reading them and making personal contributions.

F6.5 That children confirm that they can record their personal opinions and contributions to reviews, including any dissent with decisions or inaccuracies in their records.

F6.6 That children and their families are satisfied with the way in which case records are written and kept.

HOME PRACTICES

F6.7 That policy and procedural guidance for staff on case recording (and access to records) is readily available and staff are aware of its contents.

(CH Regs 15, Sch 2)
(Vol 4, 1.152ff)

F6.8 That individual case records are kept in lockable steel cabinets located in a secure part of the home.
(Vol 4, 1.153)

F6.9 That files are durable and papers are partitioned in a way that is orderly and allows for easy reference.
(Vol 4, 1.153)

F6.10 That papers which would not be open to subject access are easily identifiable within the file.

F6.11 That files allow for certificates, photographs etc belonging to the child to be kept safely.
(Vol 4, 1.153)

F6.12 That information in the individual case records conforms, as far as is practicable, to the requirements of Schedule 2 of the Regulations.
(CH Regs Sch 2)

F6.13 That entries to the record are written in a style and to a standard that is clearly expressed, free of unnecessary colloquialisms and gratuitous value judgments, and are non-stigmatising.
(Vol 4, 1.160)

F6.14 That staff actively encourage children to read their records, to correct errors and omissions, and record personal statements including any dissent the child has with decisions which affect them.
(Vol 4, 1.155, 1.161)

F6.15 That there is evidence in the records that children use and contribute to them.

MANAGEMENT ACTIONS

F6.16 That managers have provided written policy and procedural guidance on the manner in which individual confidential case records on children in homes are maintained.
(CH Regs 15(1))

F6.17 That this guidance takes due account of the need for the record to be well ordered and permanent.

F6.18 That guidance addresses the content, required style and linguistic standards of written entries.
(Vol 4, 1.160)

F6.19 That managers have provided written policy and procedural guidance on subject access to case records maintained in homes.
(Vol 4, 1.160)

F6.20 That mechanisms exist for line managers to monitor standards of individual case records and the way confidentiality and security are maintained.

F6.21 That there are arrangements for ensuring that the content of the individual case records accompany children in the event of a change of accommodation.
(Vol 4, 1.158-9)

F6.22 That there are clear arrangements for integrating information on individual case files held in children's homes with fieldwork casefiles.

F6.23 That there are clear administrative arrangements for retaining case files for 75 years, or for 15 years after the death of a child, and which allow for reasonably convenient access. [Also I3]
(CH Regs 15(3))

1 STANDARD: Location and Design

STANDARD STATEMENT

G1 The home is designed and located in a place which is in keeping with its purpose and function.

(Vol 4, 1.58 -61)

CRITERIA

OUTCOMES FOR CHILDREN

G1.1 That children feel that the design and location of the home is suitable for them.

G1.2 That children feel that the home does not stand out and they do not feel stigmatised through living there.

HOME PRACTICES

G1.3 That facilities provided are compatible with Children's Homes Regulations 1991.
(CH Regs 4, 6, 7)
(Vol 4, 1.78ff)

G1.4 That full use of space provided is made in a way that promotes the welfare of resident children.

G1.5 That facilities and adaptations are provided to enable any children with disabilities to participate fully in the life of the home.
(CH Regs 6(3))
(Vol 4, 1.78ff)

MANAGEMENT ACTIONS

G1.6 That managers make sure that as far as possible there is an alignment between the actual use of homes, their stated purposes and functions, and their location.
(Vol 4, 1.58-61)

G1.7 That each home is in keeping with its surroundings and free of unnecessary notices.
(Vol 4, 1.59)

G1.8 That the design, layout and any adaptation of the home is in-keeping with the purpose and function of the home and allows for the provision of facilities compatible with Children's Homes Regulations 1991.

(CH Regs 4, 6, 7)
(Vol 4, 1.62-81)

G1.9 That facilities and adaptations meet the needs of any children with disabilities in order to enable them to participate fully in the life of the home.

(Vol 4, 1.78-81)

2 STANDARD: Accommodation (general), decoration and furnishings

STANDARD STATEMENT

G2 The home is maintained in good order throughout, contains good quality domestic style facilities, and provides private and common facilities for the use of children and their families.

(CH Regs 6, 7)
(Vol 4, 1.54-5, 1.57, 1.62ff, 1.71ff, 1.74ff)

CRITERIA

OUTCOMES FOR CHILDREN

G2.1 That children speak positively about the physical state of their living environment.

G2.2 That children feel that the decoration and furnishings are of the same style as found in ordinary homes.

G2.3 That children should not have to wait for a long period to use a toilet, bath, shower or wash basin.

G2.4 That children in residence for an extended period confirm that their views on decoration and furnishing have been sought.

G2.5 That children are able to report that visits from family and friends are experienced as private, easily arranged occasions which do not disrupt the rest of the home.

(In the case of homes which are refuges with certificates issued under Section 51 Children Act 1989, these visits may be arranged at premises away from the home.)
(Misc Amend Regs)

G2.6 That children are able to find space for reasonable recreational pursuits.

G2.7 That children confirm that there are domestic style facilities where they can, if appropriate, do their own cooking and laundry.

HOME PRACTICES

G2.8 That the home is adequately supplied with wash basins, baths and showers, hot and cold running water and lavatories, all of good standard and sufficient for the number of children to be accommodated.

(CH Regs 7(1))
(Vol 4, 1.69-70)

G2.9 That the temperature of the water supply is safe for use by the children, having particular regard to children with disabilities.

(Vol 4, 1.70)

G2.10 That the home is adequately lit, heated and ventilated.

(CH Regs 7(2)(a))

G2.11 That the home is kept in good structural repair.

(CH Regs 7(2)(b))

G2.12 That the home, equipment and furnishings are clean.

(CH Regs 7(2)(b))

G2.13 That the home is decorated to a standard which creates a pleasant ambience.

(CH Regs 7(2)(b))

That the home is equipped with adequate facilities for catering and laundering, including domestic style facilities for use by children.

(CH Regs 7(4), 12(4))

G2.15 That the home provides a telephone where it is possible for children to make and receive calls in private without reference to staff. [Also B3]

(CH Regs 7(5))

G2.16 That the home provides rooms for children to meet privately with parents and others. [Also B3]

(CH Regs 7(3))

(In the case of homes which are refuges with certificates issued under Section 51 Children Act 1989, these facilities may be at premises away from the home.)

(Misc Amend Regs)

G2.17 That the home provides domestic style dining, lounge and recreation rooms which allow for choice, varied activities, and positive shared experiences.

(Vol 4, 1.71)

G2.18 That the home contains furniture of a style which could be found in ordinary domestic settings, and appropriate to the age of children being accommodated.

(Vol 4, 1.71)

G2.19 That the home has a means of including children in decisions about furnishing and decoration in those parts of the home shared by children.

(Vol 4, 1.71, 1.73)

MANAGEMENT ACTIONS

G2.20 That managers are able to demonstrate a planned programme of maintenance and capital works which will ensure the structural and decorative order of the home.

G2.21 That levels of decision-making and responsibilities for action with respect to maintenance are delegated to the head of home so as to achieve prompt attention to locally determined priorities.

G2.22 That these levels of delegation operate for the purchasing of furniture and equipment to allow sufficient scope for the home and the children to determine priorities and make real choices.

G2.23 That there are effective systems to monitor the fabric of the home and the adequacy of delegated budgets for furniture and equipment and to alert managers to the need for remedial work and/or additional expenditure.

3 STANDARD: Accommodation for individual children

STANDARD STATEMENT

G3 **Each child is provided with an area, identifiable as the child's own, which is equipped and furnished to the child's needs and reasonable wishes.**

(CH Regs 6)

CRITERIA

OUTCOMES FOR CHILDREN

G3.1 That children feel positively about their living environment.

G3.2 That children enjoy single bedrooms or sharing with others, as they prefer.

G3.3 That if children, for practical purposes, are obliged to share they confirm that this decision was arrived at in consultation with them, and that they feel they have been treated reasonably.

G3.4 That children confirm that they have choice in arranging and decorating their personal space.

G3.5 That children feel able to complain about aspects of their personal space, and that they feel these have been, or would be, taken seriously and treated reasonably.

G3.6 That children are able to entertain family and friends within their room or personal space in a way that is regulated sensitively and fairly.

(Not required in the case of homes which are refuges with certificates issued under Section 51 Children Act 1989)
(Misc Amend Regs)

G3.7 That older children in single rooms are able to lock their doors.

G3.8 That all children confirm that they can keep valued possessions safe and secure.

G3.9 That children confirm they have appropriate space in which to study and do homework. [Also E3]

HOME PRACTICES

G3.10 That the home is organised in such a way that individual children can enjoy privacy within a space which is identified as their own during their stay in the home.
(CH Regs 6)

G3.11 That the home allows children choice in the decoration of their individual space, having regard to the duration of their stay.

G3.12 That personal space for individual children is provided in a manner which enhances the overall sense of homeliness.
(Vol 4, 1.71)

G3.13 That where bedrooms are shared the arrangements meet the wishes of the children.
(Vol 4, 1.62-3)

G3.14 That children in shared bedrooms are allowed to personalise their area effectively.
(Vol 4, 1.72)

G3.15 That children have in their room small items of furniture which they possess.
(Vol 4, 1.62)

G3.16 That children can keep valued possessions safely and securely within their room.
(Vol 4, 1.72)

G3.17 That the home is clear about the policy and has practices with respect to children locking their bedrooms which balances the need for safety and security with freedom and privacy, having regard to the age of a child.

G3.18 That each child has appropriate space in which to study and do homework. [Also E3]

MANAGEMENT ACTIONS

G3.19 That managers have policies and procedures which require each home to provide personalised living spaces which meet the needs and wishes of individual children.
(CH Regs 6)

G3.20 That this requirement has been communicated effectively to each head of home.

G3.21 That budgetary procedures allow the home the flexibility to take account of individual children's preferences in purchasing.

G3.22 That there are policies and procedures which allow for the integration of a child with disabilities into the home.
(CH Regs 6(3))

G3.23 That there are effective mechanisms which allow managers to monitor the personalisation of living space in each home.

G3.24 That there is a clear policy with respect to children locking their bedrooms which balances the need for safety and security with freedom and privacy, having regard to the age of a child.

4 STANDARD: Safety and Fire Precautions

STANDARD STATEMENT

G4 **The home takes positive steps to keep children safe from the inherent risk of fire and other hazards to an extent that is consistent with the law and which is reasonable in daily life.**

(CH Regs 9, 14, Sch 1)

CRITERIA

OUTCOMES FOR CHILDREN

G4.1 That children feel physically safe in the home.

G4.2 That children confirm that they know what to do and how to escape in the event of a fire or other emergency.

G4.3 That children know what to do in the event of an accident.

G4.4 That children know what to do if they think something in the home is unsafe.

G4.5 That children confirm that any complaints about the safety of the home or its surroundings have been, or would be, addressed satisfactorily.

G4.6 That when children take medication, their account of how it is administered conforms to requirements.

G4.7 That children do not feel oppressed by safety rules and regulations or feel that notices or equipment are unnecessarily intrusive.

HOME PRACTICES

G4.8 That staff convey a proper regard for safety in the way they go about their work and interaction with children.

G4.9 That the head of home and senior staff take effective steps to ensure that written statements of safety policy, fire precautions and emergency procedures are readily available in the home, and that staff and, so far as is practicable, children are aware of procedures and action to be taken in the event of an emergency.
(CH Regs 14, Sch 1(8))
(Vol 4, 1.151)

G4.10 That the head of home ensures that the Fire Authority carries out periodic checks on fire safety equipment and that advice to the home on necessary fire precautions are acted on.
(CH Regs 14)

G4.11 That fire doors are unobtrusive and unencumbered.
(CH Regs 14(2)(b))

G4.12 That fire extinguishers are in working order, readily to hand, but not overly intrusive.
(CH Regs 14(2)(c), (e))

G4.13 That fire blankets are to hand in the kitchen.
(CH Regs 14(2)(c))

G4.14 That safety notices are in evidence where necessary.
(CH Regs 14(2)(d))

G4.15 That fire escape routes are marked, unencumbered and safe.
(CH Regs 14(2)(d))

G4.16 That smoke and fire detection alarms are in place and in working order.
(CH Regs 14(2)(c))

G4.17 That there are effective systems in place for reporting health and safety hazards in the home, and a means to achieve the speedy remedy of hazards and deficiencies.
(Vol 4, 1.193)

G4.18 That medicines are stored in a secure cabinet to which children are prevented from having access other than under the supervision of a member of staff responsible for administering medicines.
(CH Regs 9(1))

G4.19 That exceptional arrangements allow for the self administration of medicines by children which do not jeopardise their safety.
(CH Regs 9(2))

G4.20 That there are effective record keeping practices with regard to the administration of medicines, responses to accidents, fire drills and fire alarms in the home.

(CH Regs 9)
(Vol 4, 1.100-1)

G4.21 That the head of home and staff have received advice from a catering officer on food hygiene and safe kitchen practices, having regard to the need to allow children to assist or prepare their own meals.

MANAGEMENT ACTIONS

G4.22 That managers provide written statements of safety policy, fire precautions and emergency procedures.

(CH Regs 14(3), Sch 1(8))

G4.23 That these statements are communicated effectively to heads of homes and staff, and that, as far as is practicable, the children are aware of procedures and the action they should take in event of an emergency.

(CH Regs 14(3))
(Vol 4, 1.39, 1.151)

G4.24 That managers take appropriate steps to notify the fire authority of the details of homes as set out in regulations.

(CH Regs 14(1))
(Vol 4, 1.151)

G4.25 That managers reach agreement with the Fire Authority on how fire precaution in the home can be met in a way that is consistent, as far as reasonably practical, with normal, non-institutional daily living.

G4.26 That there are effective systems in place for monitoring health and safety hazards in the home designed to facilitate the speedy remedy of hazards and deficiencies.

(Health and Safety at Work Act 1974)
(Vol 4, 1.193)

G4.27 That there are effective systems in place for monitoring safety practices with regard to the administration of medicines, responses to accidents, fire drills and fire alarms in the home.

(Vol 4, 1.100-1, 1.142, 1.151, 1.193)

G4.28 That managers arrange for a catering officer to advise the home on food hygiene and safe kitchen practices having regard to the need to allow children to assist or prepare their own meals.

1 STANDARD: Staff recruitment, selection and vetting

STANDARD STATEMENT

H1 All staff in each children's home are recruited with particular care using clear and thorough selection and vetting procedures, designed to protect children, and achieve appropriate competencies and balance in the staff group.

(CH Regs 5)
(Vol 4, 1.27-30, 1.34-37)

CRITERIA

OUTCOMES FOR CHILDREN

H1.1 That children feel safe and protected in the presence of staff.

H1.2 That children feel that staff are suitable.

H1.3 That children feel they have someone on the staff with whom they can identify and communicate effectively.

H1.4 That, in respect of gender, race, culture, language and religion, the children feel that the composition of the staff group is sympathetic to their needs.

H1.5 That children confirm that there is an opportunity for them to meet and express views about applicants for posts in the home.

HOME PRACTICES

H1.6 That practices have resulted in a staff composition suitable for the purpose and function of the home, the protection of children and that the staff composition is sympathetic to the religious, racial, cultural, linguistic backgrounds and gender mix of the children.
(CH Regs 5(1))
(Vol 4, 1.27-1.37)

H1.7 That, where responsibility for recruitment to some posts is delegated to staff in the home, the agreed written procedures are followed.

H1.8 That staff in homes are conversant with procedures and practices which apply when applicants for posts visit the home as part of the selection process.

(Choosing with Care, Rec 11)

H1.9 That staff responsible for recruitment confirm that they have received training in recruitment and selection methods, and have access to specialised advice and assistance when required.

H.10 That personal files on current staff clearly indicate that checks on police records and the DH consultancy list have been completed.

(Vol 4, 1.34)

H1.11 That an analogous record is kept which confirms that the same checks have been made on all people who have regular, unsupervised contact with children in the home.

(Vol 4, 1.34)

MANAGEMENT ACTIONS

H1.12 That managers have devised clear, written recruitment procedures, including guidance on advertising posts, methods of selection and vetting of staff.

H1.13 That specific training is provided for staff responsible for recruitment and selection.

H1.14 That managers have devised selection methods for care staff which, among other things, test for aptitude, sound judgment, a realistic understanding of the needs of children, an ability to withstand personal stress, a willingness to discuss sensitive personal issues and receive support. [Also C1]

(Vol 4, 1.34)

H1.15 That staff recruitment operates within an equal opportunities policy and, as appropriate, allows for the application of genuine occupational qualification exemptions under the Race Relations Act 1976 and the Sex Discrimination Act 1975.

(Vol 4, 1.36)

H1.16 That these procedures result in balanced staff groups with appropriate competencies.

(CH Regs 5(1))

H1.17 That recruitment procedures ensure that the composition of the staff group is sympathetic to the religious, racial, cultural and linguistic backgrounds and gender mix of the children in the home.
(Vol 4, 1.36)

H1.18 That for all posts person specifications and job descriptions are used and reflect the staffing requirements of a particular home.
(Choosing with Care, Rec 2)

H1.19 That managers have devised routine administrative procedures for taking up references on potential staff, volunteers and independent visitors.

H1.20 That managers have devised reliable routine administrative procedures to check the names of probable employees, including temporary staff from agencies, against police records and the DH consultancy list. [Also C1]
(Vol 4, 1.34)

H1.21 That managers responsible for schools have devised routine administrative procedures for checking the names of probable employees against DFE list 99. [Also C1]
(Vol 4, 1.34)

H1.22 That managers have devised routine administrative procedures for making similar checks on potential volunteers, regular visitors and independent visitors who will have unsupervised contact with children. [Also C1]
(Vol 4, 1.34)

H1.23 That managers have devised routine methods to secure proof of qualifications of employees as early as possible and at least before the person is confirmed in post. [Also C1]
(Vol 4, 1.34)

H1.24 That managers have devised a method of routinely detecting gaps in the record of education and employment and other discrepancies in application forms, and seeking satisfactory explanations before appointments are offered. [Also C1]
(Vol 4, 1.34)

H1.25 That managers have devised methods of checking declared criminal convictions on application forms against information from police checks. [Also C1]

H1.26 That managers have provided clear policy and procedural guidance for assessing and supporting staff during their probationary period, identifying staff who should not be confirmed in post, and ensuring that appropriate notifications are made. [Also C1]
(Choosing with Care, Rec 36)

H1.27 That the selection procedures allow for tests of aptitude and psychological suitability when appropriate and that specialised personnel advice and assistance is available to staff responsible for recruitment.
(Choosing with Care, Rec 10, 12, 13)

H1.28 That there are clear procedures which require:

- applicants to visit the home where the vacancy exists when children are present in the company of a member of the selection panel;
- the applicants observed reactions, including the views of children, to be communicated to the selection panel.
(Choosing with Care, Rec 11)

H1.29 That managers monitor adherence to the requirements as set out in their written procedures.
(Vol 4, 1.34)

2 STANDARD: Adequacy of establishment

STANDARD STATEMENT

H2 **There is an adequate number of sufficiently experienced and qualified staff in the home to achieve its purpose and function and meet the needs of children.**

(CH Regs 5(1))
(Vol 4, 1.28)

CRITERIA

OUTCOMES FOR CHILDREN

H2.1 That children have a reasonable choice as to whether they relate to male or female staff.

H2.2 That children confirm that they are able to engage in purposeful activities appropriate to their age, gender and personal needs and wishes.

H2.3 That children confirm they are adequately supervised having regard to their age and competence.

H2.4 That children confirm they feel staff are competent in the jobs they do.

HOME PRACTICES

H2.5 That the actual staffing complement, in terms of numbers, grades, experience and qualifications conforms to the prescribed expectations of external managers.
(CH Regs 5(1))
(Vol 4, 1.28-30)

H2.6 That staff are deployed in a manner which best supports the purpose and function of the home.

H2.7 That the observed operation of the home confirms the adequacy of the staff complement to fulfil the declared purpose and function of the home.

H2.8 That staff are qualified to practise the methods purported to be used within the home.
(Vol 4, 1.30)

H2.9 That staff are sufficiently experienced and mature to deal with the needs of the children for whom the home is designed to cater.

H2.10 That staff believe the overall staffing complement (numbers, grades, experience and qualifications) is adequate to support the purpose and function of the home.

H2.11 That staff confirm that the impact of any staffing shortfall is addressed promptly.

H2.12 That children are adequately supervised.

H2.13 That staff are competent, and sufficient in number, to engage in activities with children appropriate to their age, gender and personal needs.

MANAGEMENT ACTIONS

H2.14 That the staffing complement, in terms of numbers, grades, experience and qualifications, is sufficient to enable the home to fulfil its purpose and function.
(CH Regs 5(1))

H2.15 That managers are able to demonstrate a rational approach to determining staff requirements.

H2.16 That managers are able to provide an accurate picture of current staffing numbers, grades, qualifications and experience.

H2.17 That managers are aware of any shortfall between staff requirements and actual staffing levels for each home, in terms of numbers, grades, qualification and experience.

H2.18 That managers are able to describe the process through which identified staffing shortfalls are addressed.

H2.19 That, where significant shortfall has been identified, managers are able to demonstrate planned actions to ameliorate its impact on practice.

3 STANDARD: Training and Staff Development

STANDARD STATEMENT

H3 Children are looked after by staff who are trained in the skills required to meet their needs.

(Vol 4, 1.30, 1.31-3)

CRITERIA

OUTCOMES FOR CHILDREN

H3.1 That children convey confidence in the staff team.

HOME PRACTICES

H3.2 That individual staff confirm that they have received induction training and that they are taking part in an ongoing staff development which meets their particular programme needs.
(Choosing with Care Rec 59, 60, 61 & 65)

H3.3 That staff express a realistic awareness of the skills and knowledge they possess and what they need to acquire.

H3.4 That staff confirm that training is available on the specific issues listed at H3.13

H3.5 That volunteers approved to work in the home have received appropriate training, particularly in relation to child protection and dealing with allegations and complaints.

H3.6 That the staff team possess the skills and knowledge required to work with the children looked after given the purpose and function of the home.
(CH Regs 5(1))

MANAGEMENT ACTIONS

H3.7 That managers have an effective, on-going training and staff development programme to maintain proper levels of skill and knowledge within the staff group of the home.
(Vol 4, 1.31)
(Choosing with Care Rec 59, 60, 61)

H3.8 That this programme includes clear expectations of induction training for all staff, with a basic minimum requirement for temporary staff.

H3.9 That this programme specifies training requirements for volunteers working in the home.

H3.10 That this programme is linked to staff recruitment information and staff supervision so as to identify staff training needs.
(Vol 4, 1.38)

H3.11 That this programme is pro-active in instituting training and staff development activity that is indicated by policy and other external determinants.

H3.12 That there are clear lines of responsibility for identifying and linking training need with training programmes.
(Vol 4, 1.45)

H3.13 That in particular there are programmes of training which address the following:

- basic residential child care skills and team working;
- specific child care approaches and skills appropriate to the home's purpose and function;
- positive means of control;
- permitted and prohibited disciplinary measures;
- child protection;
- issues of race, religion and culture;
- dealing with sexuality;
- health education relevant to growing children;

- the implications of HIV and AIDS for looking after children;
- communicating with children, including those with disabilities;
- health and safety at work, including food hygiene and safety with medicines;
- fire precautions;
- first aid

4 STANDARD: Staff supervision and support

STANDARD STATEMENT

H4 **All staff, including domestic staff and head of home, are properly accountable and supported.**

(Vol 4, 1.42 1.38)

CRITERIA

OUTCOMES FOR CHILDREN

H4.1 That children perceive staff as knowing what to do in relation to aspects of running the home.
(Vol 4, 1.39)

H4.2 That children perceive staff as confident.

HOME PRACTICES

H4.3 That all staff confirm that they have received written job descriptions which state clearly the duties currently expected of them.
(Vol 4, 1.39)

H4.4 That staff are able to give an accurate account of their role and duties.

H4.5 That staff can confirm that they have received additional written guidance, appropriate to the purpose and function of the home, which they find helpful, and which they comply with.
(Vol 4, 1.39)

H4.6 That all staff receive supervision from line managers not less frequently than every three weeks.
(Vol 4, 1.42)

H4.7 That supervision addresses the following issues:

- responses to children
- methods of working with children
- degree of personal involvement
- staff feelings and concerns
- staff development and training

H4.8 That heads of homes confirm feeling adequately supported, and can describe the way in which they are held accountable for their actions.

H4.9 That child care staff confirm feeling adequately supported, and can describe the way in which they are held accountable for their actions.

H4.10 That domestic and support staff confirm feeling adequately supported, and can describe the way in which they are held accountable for their actions.

H4.11 That there is an effective link between supervision and the identification of staff development and training needs.

H4.12 That staff meetings are held regularly at times which enable the best possible attendances.

(Vol 4, 1.46)

H4.13 That staff meetings are experienced as supportive, instructive and contribute to the cohesiveness of the staff group.

MANAGEMENT ACTIONS

H4.14 That all staff have written job descriptions which specify duties accurately, are up to date, and are subject to a process of periodic review.

(Vol 4, 1.39)

H4.15 That staff should be provided with written guidance on procedure and practice appropriate to each home.

(Vol 4, 1.39ff)

H4.16 That there are mechanisms for ensuring that this written guidance is kept up to date.

H4.17 That suitable arrangements exist for management supervision of the head of each home.

H4.18 That there are clear mechanisms of accountability of the head of each home to an external line manager.

H4.19 That managers have produced a written statement defining the expectations of the heads of homes for providing supervision of all staff in each home.

H4.20 That managers have established clear lines of accountability to the heads of homes for all staff in each home.

H4.21 That there are effective mechanisms for ensuring that managers' expectations for staff supervision are met.

H4.22 That managers have indicated how staff meetings in homes are to be facilitated, having regard to staff rotas and other exigencies.
(Vol 4, 1.46)

H4.23 That managers have taken into account the need for external consultancy in determining staff support systems, including, in particular, the needs of the head of home.
(Vol 4, 1.47-8)

H4.24 That managers are able to demonstrate a system for identifying the training needs of staff in the home.
(Vol 4, 1.43ff)

I ASPECT OF CARE : Organisation and Management

1 STANDARD: Organisation and Management

STANDARD STATEMENT

I1 **Staff in homes are organised and managed in a manner designed to deliver the best possible child care within the resources available.**

(Vol 4, 1.49)

CRITERIA

OUTCOMES FOR CHILDREN

I1.1 That children know who is, and will be on duty, and who is in charge at any particular time.

I1.2 That children feel free to make relationships with all members of staff but that they are also aware of any individual member of staff with particular responsibility for them.

I1.3 That children feel safe and adequately looked after overnight.

HOME PRACTICES

I1.4 That heads of homes are clear about the level of delegation and responsibility for:

- staff deployment
- staff supervision and performance
- staff training and development
- local budgets and financial management
- staff recruitment including the use of volunteers and agency staff

I1.5 That there are clear arrangements for identifying the person in charge of the home at times when the head of home is absent.
(Vol 4, 1.49)

I1.6 That staff rotas ensure a sufficient staff presence at key points of the day and night, and are concentrated at periods when children are in the home.

(Vol 4, 1.49)

I1.7 That heads of homes arrange for staff to be on duty at night, whether awake or sleeping in, in accordance with rules which take account of the needs of children and the purpose and function of the home.

(Vol 4, 1.50, 1.67)

I1.8 That heads of homes actively plan the workloads of individual staff.

I1.9 That staff are aware of their responsibilities and have a job description which sets these out.

(Vol 4, 1.39)

I1.10 That the responsibility of individual staff for particular children has been clearly established by the head of home.

(Vol 4, 1.52)

I1.11 That the home has developed explicit practices for handing over responsibility at shift changes, and that these address the dynamics of staff and children as well as factual information.

(Vol 4, 1.51)

MANAGEMENT ACTIONS

I1.12 That managers have set the conditions to enable heads of homes to manage the staff and other resources made available to them, and that heads of homes are held accountable for their management performance.

(Vol 4, 1.49)

I1.13 That managers have a mechanism to supervise and monitor the management practices and performance of heads of homes.

2 STANDARD: Administrative Records

STANDARD STATEMENT

I2 Administrative records contain all significant information, decisions and actions relevant to the running of the home.

(CH Regs 17, Sch 3)

CRITERIA

OUTCOMES FOR CHILDREN

I2.1 That children feel that all records which concern them are maintained securely.

I2.2 That children think that all records are accurate.

I2.3 That, in so far as it concerns them, children believe the daily log to be a fair, complete and accurate record of events.

HOME PRACTICES

I2.4 That records systems (files, indexing systems, log books etc.) are kept in an orderly manner.

I2.5 That there is an effective system for recording children's money and valued personal possessions held in safe keeping.
(CH Regs 17, Sch 3 (7), (8))

I2.6 That any record specified in Schedule 3 of the Children's Home Regulations 1991 can, in normal circumstances, be produced immediately on request.

I2.7 That all record entries are legible, signed and dated.
(Vol 4, 1.164)

I2.8 That record entries are up to date.
(Vol 4, 1.164)

I2.9 That all recording systems make use of clear, non-stigmatising, non-colloquial language.

(Vol 4, 1.160, 1.164)

I2.10 That the daily log records the actions of staff as well as those of the children in the events described.

MANAGEMENT ACTIONS

I2.11 That managers ensure and can demonstrate that homes maintain records in accordance with regulations.

(CH Reg 17, Sch 3)
(Vol 4, 1.164)

I2.12 That there are systems for external managers to:

- monitor the quality of these records;
- monitor the incidents, decisions and actions taken within homes;
- take action where necessary.

I2.13 That managers have a system for ensuring that records of menus are kept for one year and that other administrative records are kept for 15 years.

3 STANDARD: Home administration

STANDARD STATEMENT

I3 **The home is properly and efficiently administered.**

CRITERIA

OUTCOMES FOR CHILDREN

I3.1 That children confirm that their pocket money is administered fairly and efficiently.

I3.2 That children confirm that if they need information or papers held within the home's record system it can be retrieved efficiently.

I3.3 That children confirm that their money and valued personal possessions can be held securely.

HOME PRACTICES

I3.4 That a copy of the Children's Homes Regulations and associated guidance is kept in the home and is readily available to staff, children and persons with parental responsibility for children.
(CH Regs 18)

I3.5 That the head of home has received procedural guidance on exceptional access to records.
(CH Regs 15(2), 16)

I3.6 That staff in homes, including administrative staff, are aware of the need to record and notify significant events over and above what is routinely required.
(CH Regs 19)

I3.7 That the head of home is able to cope with administrative requirements and workload.

I3.8 That any administrative, secretarial or clerical staff are able to cope with administrative requirements and workload.

I3.9 That there is an effective system for holding in safe keeping children's money and valued personal possessions.
(CH Regs 17, Sch 3 (7), (8))

I3.10 That there is an administrative system for giving children pocket money which is fair, consistent and in accordance with regulations on disciplinary measures.

MANAGEMENT ACTIONS

I3.11 That managers ensure that any delegated administrative responsibilities are clear and understood by the head of home.

I3.12 That managers ensure the home has clerical and secretarial support needed to carry out administrative tasks including:

- formal notifications of significant events, admissions and discharges; [Also C3]
- written preparation for planning meetings and reviews; [Also F1 and F2]
- maintaining and updating records and written statements required by regulations; [Also A1, B1 and I2]
- financial accounts for the home and children;
- maintaining orderly, secure and accessible records and record systems. [Also F6]

I3.13 That managers have established mechanisms to monitor the performance of the home with respect to delegated administrative responsibilities.

I3.14 That managers ensure that a copy of the Children's Homes Regulations and associated guidance is kept in the home and available to staff, children and persons with parental responsibility for children.

(CH Regs 18)

I3.15 That managers ensure that there are mechanisms for the formal notification of significant events which may occur in the home in accordance with Regulation 19 of the Children's Homes Regulations 1991. [Also C3]

(CH Regs 19)

I3.16 That managers have issued procedural guidance for dealing with exceptional access to records occasioned by:

- the exercise of statute, including the powers of the Secretary of State;
- any court order;
- a Guardian ad Litem.

(CH Regs 15(2), 16)

I3.17 That there are clear administrative arrangements for retaining case files for 75 years, or for 15 years after the death of a child, and which allow for reasonably convenient access. [Also F6]

(CH Regs 15(3))

4 STANDARD: Monthly Visits by the Responsible Authority

STANDARD STATEMENT

I4 **The responsible authority receives each month, directly from the appointed visitor, a written report on the conduct of the home.**

(CH Regs 22)
(Vol 4, 1.170)

CRITERIA

OUTCOMES FOR CHILDREN

I4.1 That children confirm that monthly visits are conducted in a manner which respects them.

I4.2 That children confirm that these visits provide an opportunity to raise any concerns they may have with the responsible authority.

I4.3 That children feel that the visitors listen to them.

HOME PRACTICES

I4.4 That staff in the home confirm that monthly visits on behalf of the responsible authority take place unannounced.
(CH Reg 22)
(Vol 4, 1.170)

I4.5 That staff confirm that these are conducted in a manner which respects children and staff.

I4.6 That staff feel that these visits provide an opportunity to raise any concerns they may have with the responsible authority.

MANAGEMENT ACTIONS

I4.7 That managers have a clear policy and procedural statement, developed and authorised by the responsible authority, which sets out the arrangements for meeting Regulation 22 of the Children's Homes Regulations 1991 (as amended) and associated guidance.
(CH Reg 22)
(Vol 4, 1.170)
(Misc Amend Reg 93)

I4.8 That copies of monthly reports for the preceding 6 months are available for inspection.
(Vol 4, 1.170)

I4.9 That reports are handed direct and unchanged from the appointed visitor to the responsible authority.
(Vol 4, 1.170)

I4.10 That the responsible authority has issued guidance to the appointed visitors on the purpose of unannounced visits, the items to be covered, including offering the opportunity for private discussion with children and staff.
(Vol 4, 1.170)

Printed in the United Kingdom for HMSO
Dd 299823 C35 9/94 13110